Roger Fritz

is a planning and development consultant with fifteen years of experience in the corporate, not-for-profit, government and higher education sectors. His consulting practice combines organizational planning and development with individual career development. This combination provides a unique perspective on organizational values, vision and mission as they relate to the personal career and life aspirations of people within the organization. He is the founder of Leadership By Design, Inc., Lifeworks, Inc. and the Aspiring Organization.

He has worked successfully with hundreds of executives, managers and practicing professionals in virtually all career fields. He is recognized as an innovator in the application of psychological type to a broad range of specialities including career and management development, leadership and organizational development, as well as operational planning, strategic planning and visioning. Some current clients include Institute for Alternative Futures, Monsanto Company, IMSA - a division of Dun & Bradstreet, City of Kansas City, Professional Services Marketing Association, and the Bi-State Development Agency.

SHARPEN YOUR COMPETITIVE EDGE

Re-examine Your Instincts and Habits in Solving Problems

SHARPEN YOUR COMPETITIVE EDGE

Re-examine Your Instincts and Habits in Solving Problems

Roger Fritz

PUSTAK MAHAL®
Delhi • Bangalore • Mumbai • Patna • Hyderabad

Published in India in arrangement with **Inside Advantage Publications**

Publishers
Pustak Mahal®, Delhi

J-3/16 , Daryaganj, New Delhi-110002
☎ 23276539, 23272783, 23272784 • *Fax:* 011-23260518
E-mail: info@pustakmahal.com • *Website:* www.pustakmahal.com

Sales Centres
10-B, Netaji Subhash Marg, Daryaganj, New Delhi-110002
☎ 23268292, 23268293, 23279900 • *Fax:* 011-23280567
E-mail: rapidexdelhi@indiatimes.com

Branch Offices
Bangalore: ☎ 22234025
E-mail: pmblr@sancharnet.in • pustak@sancharnet.in
Mumbai: ☎ 22010941
E-mail: rapidex@bom5.vsnl.net.in
Patna: ☎ 3094193 • *Telefax:* 0612-2302719
E-mail: rapidexptn@rediffmail.com
Hyderabad: *Telefax:* 040-24737290
E-mail: pustakmahalhyd@yahoo.co.in

ISBN 81-223-0925-9

1st Indian Edition : January 2006

Printed at :

Contents

Introduction .... *ix*

Chapter 1: What Tools Do You Need? 1

Chapter 2: Test Your Assumptions 19

Chapter 3: Anticipating Problems with Planning 35

Chapter 4: Find and Keep the Right People 49

Chapter 5: What Makes People Perform? 59

Chapter 6: Bring Out Their Best 71

Chapter 7: Response to Pressure 85

Chapter 8: Reaction to Rejection 91

Chapter 9: The Sources of Confidence 103

Chapter 10: Failure Is Not Fatal 113

Chapter 11: Sharing the Load 129

Chapter 12: The Team Approach to Solving Problems 145

Chapter 13: Measuring Progress 161

From Now On . . . Position Yourself 175

Index *177*

Introduction

I have always thought of myself as a competitor. My earliest recollections confirm that I welcomed a challenge and liked to play with the "big boys." But, in recent times, my definition has expanded outwardly as I observed the rush toward dependency. The freedoms nurtured by our ancestors have yielded fewer and fewer people who produce added value, and experience satisfaction in their work, while more and more complain about the inconvenience and stress of making a living.

- Too many people refuse to move to find a better job.
- Too many hourly employees rely on seniority versus performance.
- Too many salaried employees resist training to enlarge their skills.
- Too many professionals rely on their credentials, status or authority versus accomplishments in meeting client needs.
- Too many teachers refuse to abandon the outdated and unnecessary protections of the tenure system and are ineffective.
- Too many physicians become so preoccupied increasing their income that their patients are neglected.

- Too many executives yield to the temptation to line their own pockets at the expense of employees, customers and stockholders.
- Too many managers resist the changes dictated by technology and global markets.
- Too many lawyers press for ridiculous settlements of cases by manipulating juries and finding legal loopholes. When they get rich doing that, they run for public office and complicate even more lives.

Millions complain about overwork. But watch them on vacation. They get more exhausted "having fun" than working.

Bottom line:

Entitlement yields idleness.
Idleness yields dependence.
Dependence brings collapse.

Work in a competitive setting is vital to economic freedom. It is the foundation on which all free societies must be built. It is the essential ingredient which makes philosophies relevant, religions meaningful and life sustainable. To defy its essence is to court personal failure and collective disaster. We are moving rapidly in the direction of both.

Americans have become infected by a something-for-nothing mentality. Wherever you look you find people thinking they can get rich without working, cheat on their taxes and get "free" government programs that someone else will pay for. The most reliable political rule for success is to perpetuate dependence on government benefits.

The surest way to reverse this trend is to increase the number of people who can compete effectively. If future generations are to benefit as we have, we must see clearly the components of being competitive *continuously*. The objective of this book is to provide tools to be competitive under these real-world conditions:

A Competitor Is:

- **An anticipator** – those who scan the horizon for trends can usually make the first move to capitalize on them.
- **A planner** – ideas which are not reduced to written objectives usually are not executed.
- **An analyzer** – disorganized thoughts indicate a disorganized mind and poor results.
- **An initiator** – when you wait for someone else to start, you may never gain an advantage.
- **An insister** – to challenge when you believe you are right is the first step to bring out your best.
- **A persister** – when you are easily discouraged you lose to those who don't quit . . . every time!
- **A recoverer/regainer** – bouncing back from a loss is absolutely essential for those who want to be around for a long time.

- **A renewer** – dependence on outside sources to improve yourself does not work. Only you can be sure you will change.
- **A reacher/stretcher** – accomplishment of routine goals yields confidence. Accomplishment of stretching goals yields excellence.
- **A persuader** – no one can read your mind. You must explain in ways which will motivate others to follow.

Now let's test your tools.

Roger Fritz

CHAPTER 1

What Tools Do You Need?

> The key to having
> a competitive edge
> is to keep learning.

Make Yourself Needed

At a dinner party recently, a friend of a friend asked me an interesting question. "They tell me," he said, "that you are a management consultant . . . just what does that mean? . . . what exactly do you do?" I recall saying something about providing an outside, objective analysis of problems faced by CEOs and their key executives; but the question lingered for days and I finally faced up to the truth. What I've been doing the past 32 years is trying to help clients ***Sharpen Their Competitive Edge*** – as organizations and as individuals. This is what I have been advising my clients to think about and guiding them to accomplish.

The most fundamental concept involved in this never-ending process is to **make yourself needed.**

It focuses on these five basic principles:

- **To avoid deciding is to invite failure.**
- **Know yourself best.**
- **Be accountable.**
- **Get time on your side.**
- **Make change your ally.**

Let's take them one at a time:

1. To avoid deciding is to invite failure.

Success is 1% luck
and 99% making
difficult decisions.

The most important question underlying decisiveness is: "What is the evidence?" When faced with decisions dealing with people, they must be able to see evidence of your support in helping them succeed. Adequate time must be allotted to plan *with* them, not *for* them; and you must be able to disagree without being disagreeable. Finally, simplicity in presenting the facts will help them perform to the best of their ability and sometimes beyond.

Periodically, it is important to change your ways of doing things. If you always do what you've always done, you'll always get what you've always got! If I was King for a day, I would put these words at the entrance of every company.

How many people do you know who "fell into a jar of jam?" I thought I had a few years ago when I bought some stock for under one dollar and in a few years it split three times and went to $44. But I didn't sell. It went down to $10. If I would have sold all of my shares at the peak, I would have made more in that one transaction than I had saved over 35 years to that point. Greed is a terrible weakness!

To sharpen your competitive edge, it is necessary to periodically complete a self appraisal inventory. Successful professionals evaluate themselves before their boss does. They never wait to be fired. Don't stay indefinitely in a job where you aren't challenged, improving and growing.

2. Know yourself best.

> You can't change others until you know yourself best.

Successful people are aware that they are not "islands." They appreciate the people behind the scenes who had a lot to do with helping them.

It is always important not to trust your own instincts exclusively without counsel. Listen to those who love you. It is sometimes painful, but too dangerous to avoid or ignore. To prove this point, if you are married, just ask yourself how many times your spouse helped you keep out of trouble?

Don't mistake rank or salary or seniority or privileges or even ownership for leadership. Owners who think they can buy loyalty are not leaders. Respect cannot be bought. It must be earned.

3. Be accountable.

Accountability precedes improvement. The never-ending quest for all competitors, at all times, in all places is to answer the question "What do we mean by performance here?"

Performance requires accountable people and accountable people always determine *who* will do *what* by *when*. This principle is being overlooked in our rush toward employee empowerment. Empowered people who will not be accountable will spin their wheels. *People* quality must come before *product* quality. Never neglect being selective about who is hired. Take more time. Be "picky." Use good selection tools. Hire the best . . . forget the rest!!

Remember: not all turnover is bad. Getting rid of your mistakes is good. Look for "bullet biters" – people who have had problems and solved them. The Japanese screened twelve times the number hired when they opened their new car plants in Illinois and Tennessee.

> The thing we call failure is not
> falling down but staying down.
> —Mary Pickford, actress, entrepreneur

Here's a little clue that will help you become more accountable – tell a few people about your commitments. The pressure you will feel to do what you said you would do is greater and will make you work harder. It tends to force action which would be easier to neglect if others didn't know about it. Also, if those who you tell about your goals offer advice, you have even greater incentive to complete them because they will want to know what happened.

It's even better, of course, if you also put goals in writing. The reason is basic and simple – **the faintest ink is better than the finest memory**.

4. Get time on your side.

> Competitiveness is
> a stream, not a spigot.
> You don't turn it on and off.

Those who try to rest on past accomplishments are almost always disappointed. It's a "what have you done for me lately" world.

Update your *Competitive Edge Profile* once a year. It's so much more useful than a New Year's Resolution. Use the simple but powerful profiling method included at the end of this chapter. It will enable you to make your personal commitment to sharpening your competitive edge.

5. Make change your ally.

> The speed of the boss is
> the speed of the team.
> —Lee Iacocca, executive

Change resisters vegetate. The ultimate proof can be found by visiting a nursing home. I recommend you do that every time you find yourself hoping things will stay the same.

Anticipation via planning is the least understood key to *organizational success*. I define planning as creating a future for your organization. If you don't plan, your future is in someone else's hands.

Look at some startling examples: General Motors lost a large share of the small car market to the Japanese. Curtiss Wright failed when it stayed with propeller aircraft, as Lockheed and McDonnell Douglas converted to jets. NCR stayed with mechanical cash registers; Addressograph Multigraph stayed with mechanical duplicators; P&G made a new detergent they called Tide. But who remembers Lever Brothers' brand called Surf?

Here are the questions to be asked:

- What is my organization doing that is no longer serving its purpose? Do I know? Do I have evidence? Am I even asking the question?

- What is my work group doing that is not cost-effective or consistent with our organization's priorities?
- What am I doing personally that may be restricting my growth, limiting my future, dulling my competitive edge?

Three words to challenge yourself – Raise the bar.

Several years ago I worked with a Senior V.P. of a $350 million retail store chain, which hoped to triple sales in five years. I asked him, "What personal development will this rapid growth require of you?" His answer, "I don't think about that. Frankly, I never thought I would get this far. I have a lot of confidence in myself so the future doesn't scare me." He was resisting self-examination and self-assessment. He was not grooming candidates to succeed him. He sealed off his future because he did not, at that lofty position with 25 years of "experience," understand that change must begin within himself. It was also interesting to note that he was the only one in the executive group who thought he was promotable.

The Challenge of Leading

> Ideas are not rare.
> Making them useful is.

Whenever you're asked to lead, the objective is the same: to achieve specific goals through the efforts of others. No matter what methods you select, your major responsibility must be to provide leadership in achieving expected results. Although this may seem relatively simple, the requirements for making it happen are demanding.

Key Factors Involved

To provide an environment in which people can perform at their best, both as individuals and as team members, leaders must:

- Plan carefully, yet be flexible and improvise when the unexpected happens.
- Introduce new ideas and procedures, yet handle the day-to-day chores required to keep the group moving forward.
- Ask the right questions – those that stimulate thinking, initiate action and foster improvement.

- Check the progress of individuals and groups to make needed changes and determine new courses of action to keep people and plans on target.
- Convince rather than dominate. This requires paying attention to and improving communication skills – listening and responding in words that are easily understood. Instead of imposing your own ideas and preferences, you will be more effective if you persuade and lead by example.

What Effectiveness Requires

> Winners mix optimism with opportunity.

Today's successful competitors are deeply committed to self-development and lifelong learning. They have taken time to study their organizations' structures, policies and objectives and clearly understand responsibilities as well as lines of authority. They are able to identify group loyalties and relationships; pinpointing growth and development opportunities for themselves and those they supervise.

Competitive leadership demands not only continuous learning, but a thorough awareness of trends and emerging patterns. To attempt to stay the same is to fall behind. Successful competitors:

- Are effective in dealing with people. They keep the organization working purposefully and harmoniously. They approach problems in an orderly way, but with a human touch. They are thoughtful, tactful and careful. As they strive for improved performance, they consistently maintain the respect of those around them.
- Are self-motivated. They manage themselves and constantly develop their capabilities. They eagerly seek out new ideas and techniques.
- Understand the need for results and effectiveness vs. efficiency. Efficient people do things right. Effective people do the *right* things right.

Identify key result areas and measures of progress. Split-second decision making is not a requirement. The best competitors think through what must be done, then take the necessary action.

The best competitors differentiate between reality and wishes. Reality requires knowing the difference between:

- Facts and opinions.
- Seniority or credentials and performance.
- Results and activities.
- Negotiation and orders.
- Written goals and good intentions.

Rate Yourself as a Competitor

Here is a concise way for you to (1) visualize the four major areas involved in being competitive and (2) evaluate your involvement and performance in each.

In the following exercise, rate your involvement in each area, using this scale:

1- Never
2- Infrequently
3- Frequently
4- Daily or almost daily

Then rate your performance in each area as follows:

1- Seldom satisfactory
2- Sometimes satisfactory
3- Satisfactory
4- Very satisfactory

Area I. MANAGING WORK
(The Results Framework)

- Strategic Plans, Priorities
- Managing for Results

1. Role and Mission – Key areas/ priorities for results: Clarification, Consensus, Commitment
2. Relating Objectives to resources
3. Objectives and Results to be accomplished in priority areas: what, where, when
4. Plans of Action to accomplish them: schedules, assignments, communication.
5. Progress Review of the vital signs to improve work and develop staff

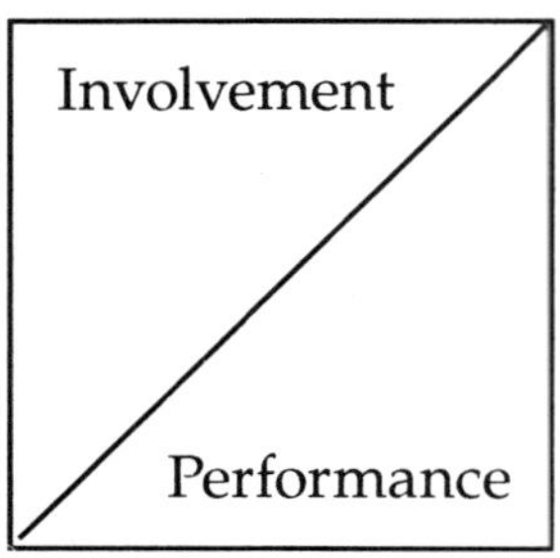

Area II. MANAGING PEOPLE
(The Human Resource Framework)

- Staffing and strengthening the Organization
- Training, Performance, Development

1. Recruitment and Selection from inside and outside the organization.
2. Induction and on-the-job training to meet work requirements.
3. Progress evaluation using work objectives and action plans.
4. Performance and Potential – their assessment, improvement, and development.
5. Succession and Replacements – finding new people who are ready, qualified, and available.

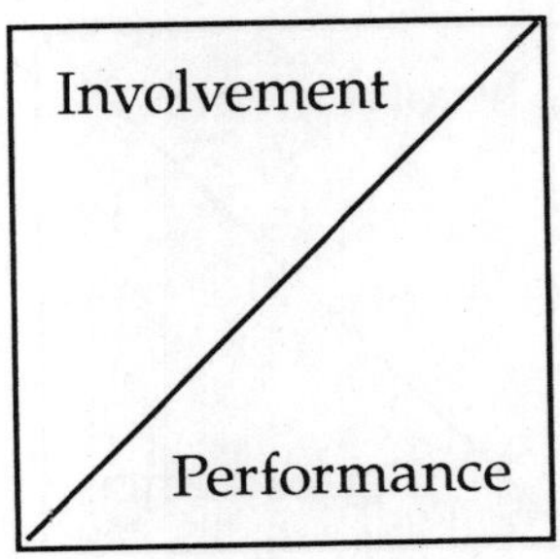

Area III. MANAGING RELATIONS
(The Interpersonal Framework)

- Communicating with individuals and groups
- Increasing motivation, cooperation and teamwork

1. Climate-setting processes for developing trust and teamwork.
2. Building supportive relationships – helper versus critic.
3. Effective communication techniques – questioning, listening, responding.
4. Basic motivation – methods for its modification and mobilization.
5. Coaching on work-related problems.

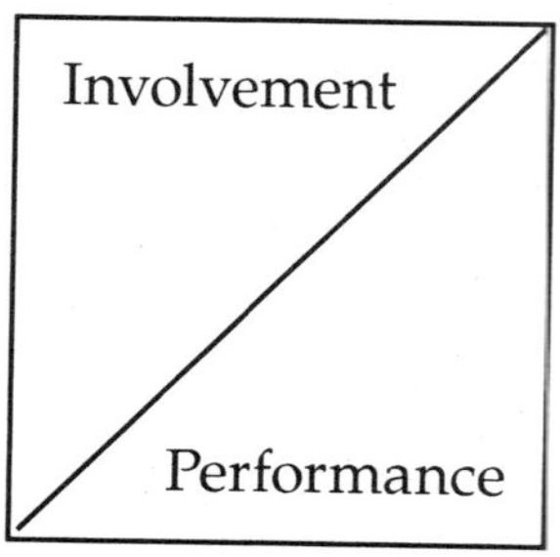

Area IV. MANAGING <u>SITUATIONS</u>
(The <u>Interaction</u> Framework)

- Handling situations and behaviors
- Problem-solving and decision-making

1. Analyzing situations – cause/effect and ends/means.
2. Changing attitudes and behaviors of individuals and groups.
3. Constructive confrontation – using it selectively and effectively.
4. Reducing and resolving conflict – methods that work and those that fail.
5. Sharing, stating and solving problems – processes, techniques, skills and applications.

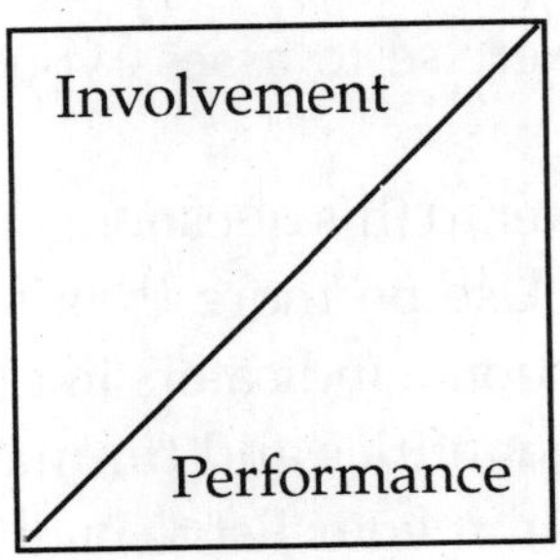

Compare the two ratings for each category. Are there categories where your involvement is high (3-4) but your performance is weak (1-2)? If so, you should target these areas for improvement. As you read through this book, think about how you might apply the techniques you will learn to strengthen your performance in these areas. If you have areas of low involvement, ask yourself why. Your job may not require your involvement in one or more of these areas. On the other hand, you may be avoiding responsibility. If so, consider how you can increase your involvement in these areas.

Performance Priorities

> Winners believe they can win.
> Losers envision defeat.

As strange as it may seem, many people don't have a clear-cut picture of what their job requires. Try this short exercise to assess your performance priorities:

Write an answer to this question: "What am I paid to accomplish?" Use no more than four words per item. Avoid directional indicators like "increase" and "satisfy." Avoid quantities and timings when listing key objectives. Limit your list to eight items.

Test your results by evaluating the items against these criteria:

- Do they represent output, rather than input?
- Are they an important part of your position?
- Do they fall within the active limits of your authority and responsibility?
- Are they few enough to assure your ability to deal with the essence of your job, yet not so few that they make planning difficult?
- Do they overlap someone else's responsibility? Or "under-lap," leaving no one responsible for the desired result?
- Do they align vertically so that your results mesh well with those above and below you?
- Do they align horizontally so that your results mesh well with those on the same level?

Are You a Competitive Leader?

> The greatest risk
> is to risk nothing.

Long ago, Peter Drucker introduced us to the concept that leaders can be identified by these qualities:

- Leaders start projects by asking, "What has to be done?" instead of "What do I need?"
- Leaders continually ask, "What are my organization's purposes and objectives?" and "What qualifies as acceptable performance and adds to the bottom line?"
- Leaders don't want clones of themselves. They never ask, "Do I like or dislike this person?" but they won't tolerate poor performance.
- Leaders aren't threatened by others who have strengths they lack.

I believe Drucker's conclusions are directly applicable to a practical current definition of competitiveness. Try it. Substitute the word competitors for leaders in each of the above statements and you will see what I mean.

CHAPTER 2

Test Your Assumptions

> You cannot compete if you are not fully committed to working hard each day. There is no vacation from excellence.
>
> —Mike Skarr, Chamber of Commerce Executive

All too often we rush into solutions without knowing first whether we are working on the most important *needs.* In this chapter, you will learn a simple but practical system to personally analyze the needs of your work group. The same method can be used later in a session with others so that you can gain the benefits of their experience and input.

Know Your Behavior Tendencies

This quiz tests your assumptions regarding people, their work, and how to get them to do the work expected. Complete it by checking the appropriate column for each of the fifteen statements before reading the explanation which follows the exercise. Follow these two simple ground rules:

- Read each statement and immediately place a check in one of the four columns. Your assumptions are being measured here, not your carefully reasoned response. Therefore, answer at once. There are no right or wrong answers.
- Think of "people" in this exercise in a general sense. Don't think of specific individuals. You are identifying the pattern of behavior, or image you project to others under normal circumstances.

Now, check the column which most closely represents your position regarding each statement. Completion should take no more than fifteen minutes.

SD = Strongly Disagree
D = Disagree
A = Agree
SA = Strongly Agree *Check One*

1. Almost everyone who really wants to can improve his or her performance on the job.
   ❑SD ❑D ❑A ❑SA
2. It is unrealistic to expect people to show the same enthusiasm for their work as for their leisure activities. ❑SD ❑D ❑A ❑SA

3. Even when given encouragement, very few people show the desire to improve themselves on the job.
❑SD ❑D ❑A ❑SA
4. If you give people enough money, they are less likely to worry about such intangibles as status or recognition.
❑SD ❑D ❑A ❑SA
5. Usually when people talk about wanting more responsible jobs, they really mean they want more money and attention.
❑SD ❑D ❑A ❑SA
6. Because most people don't like to make decisions on their own, it is hard to get them to assume responsibility.
❑SD ❑D ❑A ❑SA
7. Being tough with people will usually get them to do what you want.
❑SD ❑D ❑A ❑SA
8. A good way to get people to do more work is to crack down on them once in a while.
❑SD ❑D ❑A ❑SA
9. It weakens prestige to admit you were wrong while a lower ranking person was right.
❑SD ❑D ❑A ❑SA
10. The most effective leader is one who gets the results expected, regardless of the methods used in handling people.
❑SD ❑D ❑A ❑SA
11. It is too much to expect that people will try to do a good job without being prodded.
❑SD ❑D ❑A ❑SA

12. The boss who expects employees to set their own standards of performance will probably find they don't set them very high.

❑SD ❑D ❑A ❑SA

13. If people don't use much imagination and ingenuity on the job, it is probably because relatively few people have much of either.

❑SD ❑D ❑A ❑SA

14. One problem in asking for the ideas of employees is that their perspective is too limited for their suggestions to be of much practical value.

❑SD ❑D ❑A ❑SA

15. It is only human nature for people to try to do as little work as they can get away with.

❑SD ❑D ❑A ❑SA

Total SD	____	times 1 =	_____
Total D	____	times 2 =	_____
Total A	____	times 3 =	_____
Total SD	____	times 4 =	_____

Grand Total _____

Scoring

- Total the number of check marks in each column and place these numbers in the appropriate blanks at the end of the exercise. The totals for all four columns should add up to 15.
- Next multiply whatever total you have for each column as follows: Multiply your total

in the Strongly Disagree column by 1 and write this figure to the right; multiply your total in the next column by 2 and write this figure to the right; multiply the third column's total by 3 and the fourth column's total by 4.

- Now add up the four expanded totals. The sum of these four figures is your grand total. If you have not made any mathematical errors, your grand total is somewhere between 15 and 60.

In order to interpret your score, record it between 60 and 15 on the line provided in the figure below.

Circle your score.

60 50 40 30 20 15

Key

Ruler (60-40)
Middle (40-30)
Developmental Builder (30-15)

A "Ruler" is often called "*boss.*" He or she motivates from *fear* and supervision is *close.*

A "Developmental Builder" is often called "*leader.*" He or she motivates from *respect* and supervision is *loose.*

The theory here is that the actions of individual leaders are based on attitudes or assumptions about people and their capacity for improvement. Your set of assumptions about people and their work leads you to develop a certain style. Your score on the above scale is an indicator of your personal style. The line from 60 to 15 is intended to provide for all possible sets of assumptions regarding people and their work. Points from 60-40 represent various degrees of a ruler style, while those from 30-15 cover degrees of a developmental builder style.

The *ruler* thinks that people have little ambition, try to avoid responsibility, and want to be told what to do at all times. This leads them to assume the responsibility for setting objectives and to exercise close control. It fosters a relationship in which people are dependent, showing relatively little self-expression or responsibility. In this climate, decision-making finds little nourishment.

The Ruler:

- Says little unless something is wrong.
- Usually is not interested in the ideas of others.
- Decides what information people need.
- Changes demands unexpectedly.
- Is sometimes hard to talk to.
- Discourages people from taking risks.
- Sets objectives for people.
- Personally determines performance standards.

The *developmental builder* believes that people can enjoy work, can direct and control themselves, and will seek responsibility for their actions. Builders challenge people with opportunity and encourage them to improve. They get participation in the setting of objectives and exercise broad control that allows people to grow by monitoring themselves. They foster relationships in which people can be quite independent and self-reliant if their temperaments allow.

The Developmental Builder:

- Considers ideas that conflict with his/her own.
- Allows a reasonable margin for error.
- Tries to help others learn from their mistakes.
- Has consistently high expectations.
- Encourages people to reach in new directions.
- Helps people understand the objectives of their jobs.
- Allows people to make their own commitments.
- Sets objectives with people, not for them.

Your style probably falls somewhere along a line from the pure ruler on the one hand to the pure developmental builder on the other. The individual circumstances surrounding any action may dictate what you will do at any given moment, but the general pattern of behavior you develop over time is what will determine your place on the continuum.

Use these guidelines to interpret your score and to discover your own leadership style.

40 or higher: You probably prefer your own ideas and decisions.
31-39: You don't have any strong leanings in either direction.
30 or lower: You probably prefer involving others most of the time.

Leadership is not a popularity contest.

Does your score agree with where you thought your position would be? If not, you may not know enough about your own method of handling people, or at least don't have the same image of yourself as others do. The score on this test is probably the view others have of you.

If you are at the extreme *ruler* end of the scale (between 52 and 60), you can probably expect trouble. You apparently feel that people do not have much initiative of their own, that they have to be watched very carefully, that they have nothing of value to contribute to a group endeavor, and that they are motivated primarily by selfishness. You are likely then to be too control-oriented in directing their activities.

If you are at the extreme *developmental builder* end of the continuum (between 15 and 20), chances are you may also be in trouble. This is because you apparently do not have a sufficient sense of the need for controls. If you are too permissive in your approach to people you might well be living in the dream world of the idealist.

If you scored in the middle (30 to 35, or thereabouts), you also could have a problem. It depends on how you got this score. If you checked some answers in the first column and some answers in the last column, so that the pluses offset the minuses, then you probably do not recognize the inconsistency of your responses. A careful reading of the 15 statements will indicate that all of them really say the same thing in a different way. At the very least, you should not strongly agree with some and then strongly disagree with others. Answers running down the middle two columns, even though they are labeled agree and disagree, are really not inconsistent, given the rapidity of your response and the absence of a neutral choice.

Analyze Needs

Because results are what count, goals for an organization should be based on priorities. Goal-setting includes determining where we want to be and how we are going to get there; thus, it is necessary first of all to look at where we now are. Depending on the current situation, a particular goal may or may not be realistic; one plan of action may be more appropriate than another.

Within an organization, it is quite normal to have differences of opinion as to the current situation. Until some of these differences are reconciled, until we can agree on major assets and liabilities, until we have some consensus as to our basic purpose, we won't get very far trying to set goals that can be supported by everyone. We must start with a realistic evaluation of the present – a needs analysis.

Then we will move on to answer the question: Where do we want to be a year from now? What results would be realistic in the light of knowing where we are starting and where we would like to be?

As we look at the organization as a whole, we want to be sure there is an understanding among the key people at the top about: 1) the present and 2) the desired positions. When we move to consider goals for each unit within the organization, we will be seeking agreement among the key people at the unit level about its present and desired positions.

We want to be sure we are honestly facing up to reality – that we are not overlooking or "glossing over" important factors. Different views should be discussed, not to determine who is right or wrong, but to be as accurate as possible in identifying the most pressing needs before objectives are determined.

Your Competitive Edge Profile

> To get something you want you must look beyond the path of least resistance.
>
> —James Gray, software creator

Being a competitive leader is often frustrating and exhausting. It can also be one of the most exciting, challenging and satisfying occupations to which anyone can aspire. The key is how you answer the questions on the following pages:

Competitive Edge Profile

Name__________________________ **Date**________

What do I do best now? What are my best skills?

What is preventing me from achieving my career objectives?

Where am I most vulnerable now? Why?

In priority order, what are my three greatest needs now?

1.

2.

3.

Where do I want to be in three years?

Job Changes

Home/Family Changes

Income Changes

Location Changes

Career Changes (Education – New Skills)

New Relationships

I have identified these changes I must make to sharpen my Competitive Edge.

Change Required	Expected Result	By When	Help Needed (if any)	From Whom?
1.				
2.				
3.				
4.				
5.				

I have identified these areas of personal strengths which will enable me to sharpen my Competitive Edge.

Strength	Recent Evidence/ Proof	Confirmed by Whom?	When?
1.			
2.			
3.			
4.			
5.			

continued

At this time, I would rate my Competitive Edge in achieving my career objectives at
(1 low – 10 high).

Within 1 year, I expect to improve this rating to
(1 low – 10 high).

OR

❑I can't rate myself because my career objectives are not clear in my own mind.

The first thing I must do to be more competitive is

I must take this first step by________________.
Date

I believe I can count on ______________ to help me.
Name(s)

I realize that none of these changes will take place unless I make them happen – and I will!

_______________________ _____________

Signature Date

Tilt the Scales in Your Favor

Using this chapter to test your assumptions will enable you to move ahead steadily with greater confidence. Your *Competitive Edge* will be sharper because you have anticipated consequences and barriers. Lifetime competitors learn to tilt the scales in their favor because they:

1. minimize their resistance to change.
2. consider more options before reaching decisions.
3. realistically examine strengths and weaknesses.
4. remove obstacles or work around them.
5. control anger which alienates helpers.
6. oppose immoral behavior.
7. find trustworthy allies.
8. prioritize goals and tasks.
9. refuse to allow procrastination to determine their fate.
10. commit to continuous improvement.

> The challenge for those who want to be competitors is to be honest with themselves.

I will not allow circumstances to
determine my success;
I will make things happen.

CHAPTER 3

Anticipating Problems with Planning

I cannot control what lies ahead
for me but I can influence it
far more than anyone.

Are You Ready to Plan?

Effective planning is making a commitment to your future rather than just letting things happen. It is naïve, of course, to think that everything can be anticipated and controlled, but evidence indicates overwhelmingly that chance favors those who are prepared.

The chances of finding a better example of how to prepare for success than basketball coach John Wooden are slim to none. Considered the most successful coach in college basketball history, Wooden's UCLA teams won seven straight NCAA titles and ten overall. He won a record 88 straight games; had four undefeated seasons and became the first person to be elected to the Basketball Hall of Fame as both a player and a coach.

Wooden believed in concentrating on what he could control – his team preparation (planning) and conditioning – he spent 2 hours each morning planning the practice for that day.

- he kept notes on every practice
- he devised drills for each individual player

Players came to believe that many games were easier than practices. "The goal," he says, "is to get the most out of each person's abilities" and that happens only if they "pay the price" in preparation and hard work.

Before you determine which planning skills you need most, it would be wise to first check where you are now. Try this 10 item quiz. Score each question on the following scale:

10-9: Definite Strength
8-7: Moderately Effective
6-5: Average Performance
4-2: Rarely Effective
1-0: Definite Weakness

- Do I have a plan for spotting problems in the regular workflow and for starting remedial action? Score 1-10: _____
- Have I set up checkpoints for monitoring work in progress? Score 1-10: _____

- Am I prepared to give answers regarding the work being done? Score 1-10: _____
- Do I have a grasp of possible problems involved in making changes in procedures or routines? Score 1-10: _____
- Do I work out deadlines and stick to them? Score 1-10: _____
- Do I block out schedules coordinating shared work responsibilities? Score 1-10: _____
- Do reports indicate excessive overtime, failure to meet schedules, or serious complaints? Score 1-10: _____
- Does my group have frequent unexplained crises? Score 1-10: _____
- Have I trained someone to take my place? Score 1-10: _____
- Can I evaluate accurately the potential and limitations of people I supervise? Score 1-10: _____

If your total score is:

90-100: Planning is a definite strength.
70-89: You are moderately effective in planning.
50-69: Your planning performance is average.
20-49: It is likely that your planning is rarely effective.
0-19: It is time to get with it and develop planning skills.

Why Planning Is Resisted

> The best competitors have 2 great skills – pulling and pushing.

Trying to anticipate what lies ahead is not an inherent strength. Most people resist planning. Why? Because, as individuals, we are:

- Bored by the predictable.
- Anxious to be in control.
- Limited in self-confidence.
- Inclined to overlook shortcomings.
- Undecided about personal goals.
- Hesitant to change.

And, also, because, organizationally, we are:

- Preoccupied with present problems
- Intrigued by the unknown, yet afraid of the uncertain.
- Fearful about failure.
- Lacking in information.
- Pressed for time.
- Apprehensive about decisions that may be wrong.

Creating the Future

> The quickest way to fail
> is to overlook facts.

Everyone plans in one way or another. But most do it poorly. Few responsibilities receive so much lip service, and so little action, as the task of planning. Why?

- It requires a lot of behind-the-scenes digging for facts.
- Some fear the possibility that change may require extensive revisions.
- There are no guarantees of success.
- It's difficult to coordinate divergent views.
- Half-hearted implementation can stall or destroy an otherwise effective plan of action.
- Planners often do not receive the credit they deserve.

The benefits of planning far outweigh the inconveniences and frustrations involved. A soundly developed plan will:

- Provide you with a graphic "think-through" process.
- Relate objectives up, down and across an organization.

- Offer a means for measuring costs, time, involvement, people requirements, etc.
- Identify problems and obstacles as well as benefits and opportunities.
- Answer the question: "Where is it possible to go?"
- Suggest the best method for pacing oneself so that objectives can be attained in the shortest amount of time.

Practical planners have sufficient foresight to see a task in its entirety. Others tend to barge ahead, focusing on only the odds and ends of important jobs. Because planners think ahead, set priorities and measure progress, they succeed far more often than those who merely try to "get by for now."

When most people think of sewing machines, they think of the name Singer. But Isaac Singer was not the inventor. The original products were designed for industrial use but Singer's planning revealed that the real market was for home use so he adapted machines to sell to housewives. The result – every woman had to have one and millions were sold. His planning also indicated that sales would increase significantly if he allowed customers to pay in monthly installments.

Effective Planning in Four Steps

> The best leaders want to be judged by facts – the worst by emotional opinions.

Step 1: Where are you now?

The first and most important step in planning is to analyze your present situation. An effective current analysis permits you to look before you leap. Well handled, this first step can quickly develop a clear picture in which it is possible to determine:

- Problems that must be resolved before much else can be done. Example: Subway's first sandwich shop failed because it was in a bad location.
- Opportunities that others may not have seen – those that may have emerged recently or are likely to be seized by competitors. Example: Sears didn't consider Wal-Mart as a serious competitor until it was too late.
- Competitive factors that can stop you from achieving objectives – unless carefully countered. Example: Pizza Hut waited too long to begin pizza delivery service and by then Domino's dominated the market segment.
- New prospects that can contribute markedly to growth. Example: Microsoft's executives

knew that if their operating system was adopted early by IBM they could dominate their market even without Apple as a customer.

- Previous mistakes or oversights that have proved costly. Example: General Motors ignored the Japanese auto makers who were importing small cars into the U.S. until the profits became impossible to overlook. GM has never regained the lost market share.

Guesswork has no place in this process. Remember, the analysis can be no better than the sources used. Company records, previous plans, reports from teams or task forces and industry data can provide important information. Other resources include:

- Personal contacts
- Customer/prospect requests
- Product or service applications, complaints, changes
- Demographic studies
- Computer stored data
- Periodicals that report reliable surveys.

The first step is to organize information so that you (and those involved with you) can make the best use of it. After checking your information for accuracy and completeness, arrange it in order of importance to your goals. Then evaluate it against what is already known and, finally, outline possible actions open to you.

Step 2: Where Can You Go?

> **In the long run, discipline will accomplish more than bravery.**

The analysis you did in step 1 allows you to select both immediate and long-range objectives. These objectives should be:

1. Realistic
   - Will they bring about desired changes?
   - Can they be realized within a reasonable amount of time?
   - What costs are involved regarding time, money and personnel?
2. Specific
   - Does the objective specifically identify results anticipated?
   - When can the results be realized? And at what cost?
   - Are interim checkpoints acceptable?
3. Achievable
   - Are objectives sufficiently challenging?
   - Will they help to overcome problems or seize opportunities?
   - Can they contribute significantly to growth, revenues, profits, market share and return on investment?

Step 3: How Can You Get There?

> Winners make solutions.
> Losers make excuses.

Your plan should designate who and what will be required for completion. Be specific about the resources needed to achieve objectives. Establish checkpoints to keep the plan on schedule. Finally, develop alternative courses of action. The action plan, when properly prepared, provides these benefits:

- Agreement about what to concentrate on. Low priority activities can be dropped, delayed or reassigned.
- Fewer false starts or changes in direction.
- Improved teamwork.
- Fewer and less severe errors.
- Fewer excuses from people because of failure.

Step 4: How Will You Stay on Target?

To be an effective planner, you must follow up and be flexible. This means you must be prepared to modify or redirect portions of your plan as situations dictate or conditions change. To ensure realistic workloads, prepare a schedule. This provides a regular means of keeping your plan on track. You need to:

- Anticipate the time needed to meet deadlines.
- Determine if objective are being achieved on schedule.
- Check on any problem that causes a delay.
- Ensure that project deadlines remain realistic.
- Keep everyone informed of progress.

As you review the steps in the plan, answers to these questions will help keep objectives and actions in sharp focus:

1. Will accomplishing the objectives make a significant difference?
2. Will the accomplishments be cost-effective?
3. Have all steps been determined? What about sequence? Are the steps in logical order?
4. Are the right people involved? Informed? Capable? Motivated to do the best job possible?
5. Are deadlines realistic?

From Plans to Action

> Good people volunteer.
> Admired people are
> prepared when they do.

The true test of a plan is how well it works when put into action. It is always helpful to trace the process of moving from paper plans to implementation.

Interpret your plan as you go.

Every plan should be judged according to its purpose. Sometimes this requires modification, but with care. Plans are subject to change in detail, and part of nearly every plan has to be re-edited in light of more recent events as action proceeds.

Get going.

When a plan reaches the action stage, it is necessary to 1) evaluate progress in terms of quality, quantity, time and cost, and 2) schedule so that all parts fit into the whole.

There is only one direction in which you can coast . . . downhill. It takes more effort to get going than to keep going. In his book *The Technique of Getting Things Done,* Dr. Donald Laird has some excellent advice: "Don't look at a thing: start it. Don't put it off a day: start it. Don't pretend you must think it over:

start it. Don't start half-heartedly: put everything you can muster into your start."

Two more suggestions will help you overcome procrastination:

1. Commit yourself to deadlines in writing. Having promised performance by a certain date, you will find yourself much more likely to meet it.
2. Don't tackle an accumulation of work like a bulldozer. Break it up into small, measurable units, and grapple with them one by one.

Determine Deadlines.

Working back from the targeted completion date, determine what must be done today, tomorrow, next week, next month. Sequence is vital. If the nature of the job does not dictate the order in which certain things must be done, perform the most essential ones first.

Simplify.

Put tools where they can be used quickly and easily. Allow as few hindrances as possible.

Integrate effort.

In order to integrate effort, keep everyone who is involved fully briefed. Share your work. Delegate what you can to others, and cooperate with other departments.

Seek better ways.

When you have had a job in process for a reasonable period of time, take a look at it to see if there is an easier or more efficient way of doing it. Group activities so that one follows another with the least interruption and effort. An even pace, rather than a series of spurts, makes the best use of your energy.

Everett Kircher's love for skiing pushed him to build Boyne, U.S.A., the largest family owned ski resort chain in the U.S.

Kircher refused to be discouraged by a frequent lack of snow in his home state of Michigan and other locations. His persistent planning over many years resulted in the invention of a "snow gun," which became used by hundreds of ski areas around the world. The revolutionary equipment enabled him to extend the skiing season and to advertise "guaranteed skiing," which multiplied both income and profits.

His planning also indicated that to get optimum use of his properties, he should 1) add golf courses and instruction so his ski resorts could be used year-round and 2) seek convention business to assure that his hotel rooms, ski lifts and golf courses would all be filled. Good planning yielded good results.

> If I don't improve some things,
> who will know that I lived?
> Maybe a few other losers.

Chapter 4

Find and Keep the Right People

> Count on this – when the economy improves, the best people leave unless they are satisfied with the treatment they received in the bad times.

Unless a process is completely automated, the greatest competitive advantage lies with the people now working and those selected to join them. The best plans ever made will not succeed without quality people whose coordinated effort is focused on common goals.

The greatest challenge in attracting the best people available, is to know what it takes to succeed in your special situation. If, for example, the work is mostly routine and a few high-ranking people make most decisions, avoid those who want and need responsibility. On the other hand, if you believe your organization will be more competitive if you press people to be accountable, look for evidence of these behaviors:

What Successful Competitors Do

- **They are willing to take risks.** Pass over people who 1) prefer to be told what to do and 2) avoid being accountable. Seek those with the confidence to recover quickly from mistakes.
- **They are at their best under pressure.** Look for persons who have sought out difficult things to do. Never validate mediocre behavior by allowing it. Count on individuals who like to test themselves in ever-increasing areas of responsibility.
- **They can simplify complicated issues so others understand and will follow.** Examine carefully *why* they get things done. Do they count on seniority, credentials or rank vs. proven accomplishment? Do they try to make things difficult to enhance their own status?
- **They learn to systematically analyze alternatives.** Do they jump to conclusions without adequate investigation? Can they get the facts needed quickly? Do they ask the right questions? Do they involve people close to the action when solving problems?
- **They control emotional extremes neither sulking in defeat nor gloating in victory.** Is there evidence of pouting, withdrawal and blame when things go wrong? Is praise shared? Remember: Those who accomplish most believe that "the best is yet to come."

- **They qualify themselves with expertise.** Do they tend to trust their "buddies" too much? Are they willing to pay their dues in terms of study, training, testing and qualifications?
- **They sort divergent views and formulate action.** Are they able to get talented people to join them? Will able people follow their lead? Do they encourage constructive confrontation? Can they disagree without being disagreeable?
- **They discipline themselves to anticipate critical change.** Do they take the time needed to find and hire the best people available? Do they understand the importance of training and provide resources for it ***continuously***?
- **They help others succeed.** Look for people who have learned the benefits of teamwork – who have learned to multiply their own achievements by involving others whose abilities supplement and complement their own.

> Praise has a bigger payoff than selfishness because it is effortless.

- **They balance career and home responsibilities.** Don't try to take on this responsibility for someone else. Keeping life's varying demands in balance can only be done by individuals. Look for those who are succeeding or they will blame you when things go wrong.

- **They temper personal impatience with team building requirements.** Do they tend to hire people whose skills and abilities exceed their own in needed areas? Are they threatened by talented people? Do they focus more on helping the best performers improve vs. hoping the worst will reform?
- **They think of failure as an opportunity to try something new.** Favor those whose background indicates that they do not stay depressed or dejected. Talk to those who know them well. Visit them in their own territory. The key to success is to bounce back.

> Year after year, forcing managers to weed out their worst performers was the best antidote for bureaucracy.
>
> —Jack Welch, CEO of General Electric (retired)

Answer These Questions First

The best place to find useful information is in the original interview with job candidates. The keys are asking probing questions and listening carefully to the response. Here are some suggestions designed to help you accurately judge whether the person can be objective about themselves and should be considered further.

- Describe a situation at work where you think you could have done a better job. (Listen for what may sound like excuses or blaming others.)
- If I had been your supervisor this past year, what would I be saying now about your performance? (Listen for clues about basic issues vs. trivia.)
- What have you been involved with at your job that you don't ever want to do again? (Listen for evidence of what they think is either too much or too little responsibility.)
- What would you say if I told you I was not satisfied with this meeting? (Look for signs of stress and whether they can remain calm.)
- How would you describe the worst and best boss you have ever had and why? (Listen for specific examples of what they believe they learned from their contacts.)
- If I said I was going to decide whether to hire you within 5 minutes, what would you tell me? (Listen for references to how they believe their strengths match the job's requirements.)

A group of people
each going their own way
is not an organization.

The Hazards of Hiring

The best organizations find ways to minimize hiring hazards. They are always cautious, deliberate and thorough in the selection process. They find ways to address the potential problems most pertinent for them. Here are the "watch out" areas with the best payoff.

- **Mediocre people attract mediocre people . . . or worse.** Anyone can prove this point any time by looking back on the records of bad employees who recommended other bad employees. In other words, if someone rates a 5 on a scale of 10, the odds of them recommending someone above 5 are very low.
- **Slow is better.** The quicker you hire the greater the chance of error and failure. Thoroughness is important. Speed is a detriment. There are too many things which can be easily overlooked. It's easy to make a mistake by not hiring someone judged to be a failure who dealt with very difficult situations or, on the other hand, to judge as a success an individual when other people consistently made them look good or carried them on their shoulders.

  Take the time and spend the money to document everything from work history, performance record, attitude and compatibility.
- **Always look beneath the resume.** David Moore has built Corinthian Colleges, Inc. into one of

the largest for profit post-secondary education companies in the United States. They operate 69 colleges in 21 states. Moore learned leadership during a distinguished military career during which he served 3 tours in Viet Nam. There he learned the difference between taking risks versus gambling on a decision. "When someone can get killed, it makes decision making a very personal thing," he says.

To be able to count on others, Moore places the highest value on integrity and initiative. Neither of these critical qualities will appear on a resume. They take time and effort to verify but without those investigations the risks become too high.

Concentrate on proven accomplishment without unusual advantage, protection or luck. Joan Ganz Cooney encourages the people she hires to argue with her. "I like being told I was wrong. I was saved from many, many errors and wrong turns by people who argued with me and made their case," she says. When people know she will rely on their judgments and recommendations they work much harder to be accurate. Knowing that she trusts them puts a greater burden on their shoulders.

The philosophy has paid off handsomely for her. The *Sesame Street* program she created in 1968 has won 86 Emmy Awards and 10 Grammy Awards – more than any show in the history of television. She was inducted into the National Women's Hall of Fame in 1998.

- **Welcome new ideas.** Donald Douglas, who founded Douglas Aircraft Company in 1921, was one of the country's first aeronautical engineers. To build a company, he realized that he had to get a constant new flow of ideas from others. When bright people found out that he would welcome them and reward them, they were eager to sign up. Many of these aviation pioneers went on to start their own companies including John Northrup (Northrup Aviation) and James Kindleberger (North American Aviation).

  Douglas never got a pilot's license himself but was able to nurture and encourage tens of thousands of others in building one of America's most successful aircraft companies.

Ties That Bind –

Finding and Keeping Allies

The purpose of finding and keeping allies is not mysterious. Too often people who think of themselves as leaders *assume* advocates will help when needed. They are shocked to be standing alone because they failed to follow *7 basic principles*:

1. **Find common interests early in a new relationship.**
   Study their record of previous alliances. What does this tell you? Do they need you

more than you need them, or vice versa? Why?

2. **Determine the depth and scope of their influence.**
   Is their position based on shallow personal charisma with a few or a large following?
   For example, Margaret Thatcher realized in 1979 that a majority in Britain agreed with her toward individual freedom and conservative policies.
3. **Are you comfortable sharing the limelight with them?**
   Is this person a "scene stealer?" Will they "hog" the camera or "upstage" you at every opportunity? If yes, can you get what you need from the relationship anyway?
4. **Can you reach compromises which are mentally acceptable?**
   Is the person predatory or affable? Who must he/she please to stay in power?
5. **Have they proved they will be with you at the most critical time their support is needed?**
   Have they been tested? What happened?
6. **What trade-offs or sacrifices are required of you in keeping this alliance?**
   For example, by aligning yourself with this ally, do you automatically inherit new enemies?
7. **Given the pros and cons, is the risk acceptable?**
   At the end of the day, if I give my best effort,

will the relationship provide significant advantages I am not likely to get another way?

It's your move!

CHAPTER 5

What Makes People Perform?

> Forget good times
> and bad times –
> think NOW.

To compare outlook toward job conditions, the United States Chamber of Commerce conducted a study involving 40,000 hourly paid employees and 5,000 of their supervisors. Employees were asked to *rate the job conditions listed below in order of importance from 1 (most important) to 10 (least important).* Their bosses were asked to rank the same items as they believed the average employee would. To see how your views compare with theirs, please use the "Supervisor Rating" column to record your opinion as you think the average hourly paid employee in your organization would. We will then compare your ratings with those in the study.

	Job Conditions	Employee Rating	Supervisor Rating
1.	Full appreciation of work done.		
2.	Feeling "in" on things.		
3.	Sympathetic help on personal problems.		
4.	Job security.		
5.	Good wages.		
6.	"Work that keeps you interested."		
7.	Promotion and growth in company.		
8.	Personal loyalty to workers.		
9.	Good working conditions.		
10	Tactful disciplining.		

	Job Conditions	Employee Rating	Supervisor Rating
1.	Full appreciation of work done.	3	8
2.	Feeling "in" on things.	4	10
3.	Sympathetic help on personal problems.	9	9
4.	Job security.	1	2
5.	Good wages.	2	1
6.	"Work that keeps you interested."	5	5
7.	Promotion and growth in company.	7	3
8.	Personal loyalty to workers.	10	6
9.	Good working conditions.	6	4
10	Tactful disciplining.	8	7

Note the marked differences in viewpoint. The workers ranked appreciation third, for example, and promotion and growth seventh; their supervisors gave almost completely opposite responses, scoring appreciation eighth and growth third. Similarly, the workers indicated that it's much more important to feel "in" on things and receive appreciation for work done than their supervisors thought they would.

Conversely, the workers thought a lot less of "loyalty" than their bosses thought they would.

If your rankings differ significantly from those of the workers in this survey, it would be a good idea to reexamine how realistic your views are when compared to those of non-supervisors.

> Luck can sometimes happen,
> but not if you wait for it.

Basic Motivation Requirements

These factors should be present in order to create optimum conditions for motivating people to perform at their highest level:

1. Team Leaders who
   - are approachable and open minded.
   - share information *before* it's needed.
   - encourage initiative.
   - help people learn from mistakes.
   - give credit when due.
2. A process for setting goals which
   - relates organizational goals to personal goals.
   - helps people set goals and measure their own progress.
   - stresses *negotiation* of results expected in advance.

3. A leadership commitment which
   - enables individuals to achieve personal goals by achieving organizational goals.
   - can be managed by people not rule books or computers.
   - reveals a builder vs. dominant approach to leadership.

1. Which of these requirements are met in your organization?

2. Which are *not* being met?

3. Which requirements are not being met in your team?

4. What steps can *you* take to improve the situation?

How Achievers Can Lose

A desire to be competitive is not enough. You can even be an achiever and not be successful. This is because others view your success in terms of what they expect from you. The greater the expectation, the lower your success is perceived! This is expressed in the following formula:

$$S = A/E$$

Success = Achievement/Expectations

Success is the ratio of achievement to expectations. In other words, if you achieve a lot but others expect more, your success ratio is low.

Your answers to the following questions explore how your achievements are perceived and how your expectations affect others' success.

1. What does this formula mean to you personally? For example, are you achieving more or less than your spouse thinks you should? In what ways?
2. What does it mean to you in terms of your work relationships? For example, are you getting accurate feedback? Do you get both good and bad news when necessary?
3. What does it mean in terms of your relationship with your team leader? For example, are you meeting his/her expectations?

Conclusion

To compete effectively and achieve high performance over an extended period of time, people must learn to work well with minimum direct supervision.

Koch Industries, a large oil and gas conglomerate works hard to encourage employee innovation. The results are amazing – sales have reached $40 Billion and it is the second largest private company in the U.S. Examples:

- A refinery worker was told to use his judgment and experience to decide when to change a pressure valve instead of following a predetermined rule. Performance went up 20%.
- A team of employees in Minnesota volunteered to increase a pipeline capacity by 15% and saved $30 million. Each got a bonus of 15% of his salary.
- Employees initiated a study of unsafe conditions which resulted in 35%–50% improvements in the number and severity of accidents.
- An employee who was an auto racing fan developed a way to make racing fuel at lower cost than competitors.
- Because disagreement is inevitable when initiative is encouraged, that fact must be anticipated. The best way is to follow some simple guidelines.
- Don't make differences personal. Treat them as issues requiring more study.
- Relate rewards to success in overcoming differences when solutions are found.
- Provide for ways to expose conflicts before they get worse.
- Give extra rewards for fast results.

Find Your Competitive Index (CI)

How do we know if a drive to win has gone too far? When we are overly aggressive? When forcefulness is causing isolation? These questions will enable you to be more objective about your CI.

U = Usually S = Soometimes R = Rarely

	Check One
1. I need to be busy.	❑U❑S❑R
2. I get bad advice.	❑U❑S❑R
3. I recover quickly from mistakes.	❑U❑S❑R
4. People believe I am restless.	❑U❑S❑R
5. People say I am insensitive.	❑U❑S❑R
6. I associate with winners.	❑U❑S❑R
7. Losing is very stressful.	❑U❑S❑R
8. I hate to apologize.	❑U❑S❑R
9. People say I make excuses.	❑U❑S❑R
10. People say I avoid decisions.	❑U❑S❑R

Score 5 points for each ***usually***
Score 3 points for each ***sometimes***
Score 1 point for each ***rarely***

10 – 20 points = **Low CI** – You will usually find the help you need.

20 – 35 points = **Mid CI** – Assistance is unpredictable.

35 – 50 points = **High CI** – Your competitiveness discourages support.

> If you resent being on the sidelines, find a game you can play in.

Concentrate Your Energy

Here are some powerful clues to help you focus your effort to get the best return:

- Seek opportunities to perform jobs that interest you and that you do well.
- Channel your effort to increase competence in your chosen field.
- Focus on highest priorities.
- Incorporate personal satisfaction in completion of your goals.
- Delegate to effective people.
- Keep your family life and emotional support systems functioning.

T.V. star and author Bill O'Reilly believes that his success is directly due to his dedication to working hard, never missing a day of work, "never being satisfied until my work is better than what other people were putting out, and not making excuses when I flopped." Not a bad formula for anyone concentrating their energy to get ahead.

The Keys to Competitive Effectiveness

Organizational

What is the evidence:

- That I select people whose behaviors (especially their strengths) complement mine and combine to meet the demands of our job?
- That I *negotiate* objectives to make them stretching, yet realistic and attainable?
- That I am rarely surprised and can quickly find out what I need to know?
- That I can simplify (vs. complicate) issues, and am usually understood?
- That I will encourage dissenting points of view to arrive at better decisions?

Interpersonal

What is the evidence:

- That I really want to succeed?
- That I allocate adequate time to plan with you?
- That I will be calm in a crisis or emergency when others behave irrationally?
- That I encourage calculated risk, but avoid shooting the messengers of bad news?
- That I can disagree without being disagreeable?
- That I avoid the symbols of status, power and privilege, which may yield fear, isolation and suspicion of motives?

Ninety-nine percent of failures come from people who have a habit of making excuses.

Success in motivating for performance boils down to how we answer this question: can people do their best here?

Unless the answer is based on specific evidence of measurable success, excuses will prevail. Any of them will postpone the ultimate day of reckoning. The best competitors win because they don't make excuses – they perform!

Chapter 6

Bring Out Their Best

> We tend to improve when those we respect expect it.

Why Competitive Leaders Are Scarce

There is a severe shortage of leaders who are cleanly competitive and make best use of their own and others' talents to accomplish goals because:

- Almost everyone prefers to be popular rather than try to break new ground.
- Very few people have enough self-confidence to endure little praise.
- The need to be recognized is greater than the satisfaction gained from making changes – even when they are long overdue.
- Most of us retreat, wilt or explode when opponents threaten to expose our weaknesses.
- As we try to hide our mistakes we become more aware of our vulnerability.

- Our ambition allows us to compromise principles and then integrity erodes.

My conclusion is that these major themes prevail throughout the lives of true competitors:

- **They value their time**. Competitive people guard their time very carefully. They think of time as their most valuable resource. When people consistently take advantage of their time, they do not ignore the situation, but face it head on.

  Good time managers take advantage of down time to work on pending projects. They keep to-do lists religiously and are very conscientious about working on highest priorities first. They are very conscious of how time can be wasted in meetings so require agendas and time allocations for each subject covered. When meetings conclude, they evaluate them so that time is not wasted in the future repeating subjects where decisions have already been made.
- **They refocus quickly**. The best word to describe competitors is that they do not hesitate to change course. Their present situation bothers them so much they consider it worse than failing at something new. James Cook was such a man. His willingness to venture into uncharted waters transformed navigation in the 18th century via 3 year voyages mapping out vast areas of the South Pacific Ocean from the Arctic to Antarctica, including Australia, New

Zealand, Tahiti and the discovery of Hawaii in 1778.

Beginning as an apprentice seaman at age 18, he was offered command of a merchant coal ship only 9 years later at age 27. He declined in favor of joining the Royal Navy for greater long-term opportunity. His gamble was justified. Just 12 years later, at age 39, Cook was the first non-commissioned officer to ever be given command of a British Navy Vessel.

- **They maintain momentum**. Larry Bossidy has been a very successful executive for many years at both General Electric and more recently when he met the challenge of combining Allied Signal with Honeywell. Bossidy believes that momentum is achieved when there is a continuing emphasis on learning throughout an organization. He wants people to be sure that there is a linkage between the decisions they make and the action that will be taken. His reputation is that he is always asking *who* will do *what* and *when*. If you don't plan on answering those three questions about any proposal, he would prefer that you wait until those questions are addressed.
- **They raise the bar each time they succeed.** Perhaps the best known female athlete in the world, Mia Hamm is committed to overcoming any kind of complacency. She never wants to allow herself to get comfortable or confident because "that's when a weaker opponent can sneak up and knock you off your perch," she

says. For Hamm, her success boils down to a consistent commitment. Even when discouraged and exhausted, she believes she must keep improving or she will fall behind and her team will not be as good when she is not at her best.

> Celebrate what you have accomplished, but raise the bar a little higher each time you succeed.
> —Mia Hamm, U.S. Soccer star

- **They look for a challenge**. The man voted the greatest athlete of the twentieth century was first, last and always a competitor. Jim Thorpe had a very unusual beginning. Born on an Indian reservation in Oklahoma, he showed athletic interest very early. When only 10 years old, he ran home from school – a distance of eighteen miles.

During his days at the Carlisle Indian School in Pennsylvania, he attracted national attention as a track star and football player. In 1912, Carlisle was the national collegiate football champion and defeated nationally prominent football powers including Harvard, Syracuse, Pittsburgh, Nebraska, Penn State and Army. He was voted an All-American.

Later, he became the only athlete to win the decathlon and pentathlon in the same Olympics. His versatility was noted when he became the first American to simultaneously play professional football and baseball.

- **They study their opposition**. Too often, we think of competitive people as tense, emotional and quick-on-the-trigger workaholics who are always looking for a contest. That definition usually leads to trouble.

  When I see that type of person, I think of my friend, Mike Singletary. Considered one of the best linebackers ever in the National Football League, Mike is at his best helping people overcome the odds against them. His record as a Hall of Fame professional athlete is unsurpassed. His accomplishments since then illustrate exceptional skills as a speaker, motivator, trainer and coach. Fans still remember the intense look in his eyes as he stared at the opposing quarterback. I always thought he was saying to himself, "Please come my way; I'm ready. Try me." But there is much more to Singletary's competitiveness.

  - He prepared harder and longer than anyone else on the team.
  - He helped teammates whenever possible.
  - He spent more time watching opponents' films than anyone else.
  - He challenged himself first to improve before making suggestions.
  - He let his actions speak louder than his words.

Much of Mike's advice is included in his new book *The Leadership Zone,* written with his business partner, Rick DeMarco. The lessons are valuable for everyone.

- **They control unnecessary confrontation**. An honest answer to these questions will help control unnecessary confrontation. Answer each question YES or NO, then score yourself.

Controlling Confrontation

1. Can you avoid discussing "hot" subjects, such as politics and religion, when having a discussion?

   ❑Y ❑N
2. Can you make it clear where some of your thoughts are opinions, not facts?

   ❑Y ❑N
3. Do you try to avoid confrontation with those you're most inclined to disagree with?

   ❑Y ❑N
4. Do you make certain you hear the other person out before formulating a reply?

   ❑Y ❑N
5. Can you find points in the other person's views you can agree with?

   ❑Y ❑N
6. Can you back up your own viewpoints with facts and reasoning, instead of emotional outbursts?

   ❑Y ❑N

7. Do you avoid making sarcastic remarks?

❑Y ❑N

8. Can you keep your cool when someone tries to get you to lose your temper?

❑Y ❑N

9. Do you truly believe that everyone is entitled to an opinion?

❑Y ❑N

10. Do you take pride in the battles that you successfully avoid?

❑Y ❑N

How did you do on the quiz? A score of eight YES answers or more indicates that you can avoid confrontation. Since none of these questions asks the impossible, a score of seven or below probably indicates that you place "being right" above teamwork, cooperation, and mutual respect. Such an attitude may come back to haunt you later.

> There is little in life to hate
> but much to be ignored.

- **They prepare relentlessly**. Harold "Red" Grange was the best known college and professional football player of his time. He became legendary while playing at the University of Illinois, where he averaged 151 yards per game and was a three time All-American. He's credited with putting professional football on the map after he joined the Chicago Bears in 1925.

The price for success, he believed was "endless preparation," so that when there was an opportunity, he was ready.

> I didn't come into this league thinking I was one of the most talented guys. But what I did say is I wasn't going to let anyone outwork me.
> —Karl Malone, #2 scorer in NBA history

Harvey Pennick became one of the best-known golf coaches and instructors because his advice was sought by many successful professionals. Pennick based his success on his habit of recording everything he wanted to use in his coaching in a "little red book." He used that notebook to help his students adopt the methods used by the best players. The pupils were able to select from the successful techniques and use them in improving their own game. Converted into a conventional-sized book, it became a New York Times best-seller in 1992.

- **They build bridges to those who can help them**. When Arnold Schwarzenegger decided he would run for Governor of California, he realized he would need a lot of help. His background was not involved with politics.

On the contrary, he had devoted almost all of his adult life to show business in one form or another. He did, however, acknowledge how much help he had received from other people as a body builder and actor and realized that same approach would be necessary in politics. Just as he took acting and elocution lessons to overcome his accent, he determined he would seek out people with expertise who could 1) analyze the major problems in California, 2) develop constructive programs to address them and 3) plan for a series of programs, which would enable that state to regain its financial stability.

Fred Smith, the founder of Federal Express, has based his career on helping others get what they want, so that he could get what he wanted. Smith frequently visits with employees at their workplace and is quick to express his thanks for their effort. Most of his visits are not planned, so that he can tune directly into what people are doing, without knowing about his arrival in advance.

President Harry S. Truman's loyalty to his staff was well-known throughout his career. Once, when he was a captain in the army in WWI, he put a wounded enlisted man on his horse. A higher ranking officer passing by noticed Truman, the officer, walking while the enlisted man rode, and ordered the soldier to get off. Truman objected, saying, "You can take these bars off my shoulders, but as long as I'm in charge, that man's going to stay on that horse." The colonel backed off. Although Truman's expectations were high, he refused to take advantage of people.

Even when Truman was put in tough situations, he supported his people. He became president only two months after being sworn in as Franklin Roosevelt's Vice President in 1944. He was not prepared for the tremendous burden of the presidency. Truman didn't even know that the U.S. was building an atomic bomb, for example. When putting together his new cabinet, he sought people who he believed would give him their best recommendations rather than telling him what they thought he wanted to hear. Because Truman was very skeptical of critics who offered no alternatives or solutions, he would frequently shock opponents by asking them if they had a better answer. Most, of course, did not and he made his point very effectively.

- **They bring out the best in those they trust.** Even President George W. Bush's most active opponents will acknowledge that his achievements have exceeded the hopes of even his most active supporters. There is a general agreement that in the face of great domestic and international problems and adversity, Bush has been able to stay with his main ideas and not waver. His reputation is that he consults frequently with his key advisors, and encourages frank questions and responses to reduce the possibility that he will make a preventable mistake. In the critical area of national defense, for example, he has used both Donald Rumsfeld and Dick Cheney for advice because both have served previously as Defense Secretaries and in the U.S. House of Representatives.

If respect is not earned and deserved, it will melt.

Howard Schultz, founder and chairman of Starbucks Coffee Co. wants everyone to know that he considers all Starbucks employees, even those who work part-time, as stakeholders in the company. Because his original goal was to exceed his customers' expectations, he needs to have that motivation ingrained in the people who deal directly with the customers. He calls this "demonstrating the conscience of your business."

To bring out the best in people, leaders who are competitors must also understand how to use incentives for example:

- They must resist the temptation to fire people who take risks when their ideas are not 100% successful.
- They must back off from hiring and advancing people who are like them. Rather, they must balance their organization with individuals who

collectively can accomplish the work required.

- They must be tolerant of individuals who are innovative even when some of their characteristics and behaviors are different from the majority.
- They encourage people to get different ideas from competitors and other successful operations.
- They must stay in tune with those who understand the impact of listening to ideas different from your own.

Those who are able to maintain a competitive outlook over time realize that they must pay adequate attention to those who follow them. Many experts believe that the best leaders have also been good followers. They cite as examples many who have made their bosses look good.

Competitors in leadership positions must learn to multiply themselves. That is, they must learn how to gather and build teams of people with supplementing and complementing backgrounds, talents and abilities. I have summarized what I believe are the bedrock principles involved in this quest in what I call the "Competitor's Prayer."

The Competitor's Prayer

Please help me . . .

- Understand that my beliefs and standards are not shared by everyone.
- Be patient with those who are slower than me.
- Slow down those who are moving too fast.
- Get facts before opinions.
- Go on when others are discouraged.
- Set a good example of accountability.
- Look for *what* is wrong before criticizing *who* may be wrong.
- Get decisions made as close to the action as possible.
- Listen and question before making a judgment.
- Change before I have to.

CHAPTER 7

Response to Pressure

Two factors are vital in an ***objective*** self-evaluation – pressure points and results achieved.

Pressure Points Quiz

Job pressures can erode efficiency, productivity, and even your mental and physical health. You can get some indication of the degree of pressure you are feeling by taking the following quiz.

If the statement *never* applies to you, score 1; if *seldom*, 2; *sometimes*, 3; *often*, 4; or *always*, 5.

1. I'm not sure what's expected of me.
   ❑1 ❑2 ❑3 ❑4 ❑5
2. Demands for my time are conflicting.
   ❑1 ❑2 ❑3 ❑4 ❑5
3. Going to and from work is stressful.
   ❑1 ❑2 ❑3 ❑4 ❑5
4. My work is interrupted for new priorities.
   ❑1 ❑2 ❑3 ❑4 ❑5
5. My relationship with my boss is not good.
   ❑1 ❑2 ❑3 ❑4 ❑5

6. I only receive feedback when my performance is unsatisfactory.
❑1 ❑2 ❑3 ❑4 ❑5
7. I believe I have little chance for promotion.
❑1 ❑2 ❑3 ❑4 ❑5
8. Most decisions that affect me are made without my knowledge.
❑1 ❑2 ❑3 ❑4 ❑5
9. I usually have to work under unfavorable conditions.
❑1 ❑2 ❑3 ❑4 ❑5
10. I have too much to do and not enough time to do it.
❑1 ❑2 ❑3 ❑4 ❑5
11. I feel my beliefs are not shared by many people here.
❑1 ❑2 ❑3 ❑4 ❑5
12. I do not have enough work to do.
❑1 ❑2 ❑3 ❑4 ❑5
13. I worry about failure.
❑1 ❑2 ❑3 ❑4 ❑5
14. I fear those above me believe I am not qualified for my job.
❑1 ❑2 ❑3 ❑4 ❑5
15. I'm afraid someone else will soon take over my job.
❑1 ❑2 ❑3 ❑4 ❑5
16. I feel pressure from home about the time I spend at work.
❑1 ❑2 ❑3 ❑4 ❑5
17. I spend too much time on unexpected things.
❑1 ❑2 ❑3 ❑4 ❑5

18. Layoffs are likely here.

❑1 ❑2 ❑3 ❑4 ❑5

19. I don't have enough opportunity to use my knowledge and skills.

❑1 ❑2 ❑3 ❑4 ❑5

20. It seems I move from one deadline to another.

❑1 ❑2 ❑3 ❑4 ❑5

TOTAL SCORE . . . .

If your total score is under 50, you can relax and enjoy your work. The pressures are exceptionally few.

If your score is 50-60, you're experiencing normal on-the-job pressure, and there's little to worry about. When changes must be made, make them selectively.

A score between 60-70 indicates a moderate amount of pressure and indicates that some changes ought to be considered as soon as practical.

When a score ranges between 70 and 80, you are undergoing an abnormal amount of pressure, and should make some changes immediately. Between 80 and 90, pressure has reached the danger point; above 90, you had better make some prompt, major changes *at once* or you will become the proverbial "basket case."

How Pressure Will Pull You Down

Pressure is a prominent cause of energy loss and fatigue. Fight it by letting off steam to a confidant. Repressed feelings of hostility consume a great deal of energy.

Uncertainty is debilitating. Know what goals are to be achieved. Do some things that promote relaxation. Keep a sense of humor, including the ability to laugh at yourself. Recognize your personal limits and direct your energy toward positive goals.

Self-discipline is the best means of staying on the right track.

Pressure Prevention

Each individual has their own capacity for pressure and their own mechanisms for coping with it. There are no "universal" rules for helping a person deal with stress, but there are a few general guidelines that are worth consideration.

1. **Don't be crushed if you fail**. If you indulge yourself that way, you will never put yourself in a pressure situation again and you'll never grow. If you fail, go back over the situation from the moment things started to go wrong. Try to determine why. Figure it out. Then try again.

2. **Don't change your life radically when you're under sustained pressure or know you're about to be**. A pressure situation is not the time for making major changes. Wait until things calm down.
3. **You need the support and honest appraisal of your family and friends**. Embrace their help if they offer it. Ask for it if they don't.
4. **Keep it all in perspective**. You can't control everything around you, so don't try. No matter what kind of pressure you're under today, tomorrow will offer a new opportunity, a different perspective, a new cause for optimism.
5. **Do things that help you to relax**. Relaxing, stimulating, enjoyable things can do a great deal to take the edge off tension. The stressful situation may still exist, but you will be better able to handle it if you have released some of the pressure, even for a little while.
6. **Develop stamina**. Physical exercise is essential. Nutrition counts. So does a good night's sleep. But don't turn to alcohol or drugs as a means of dealing with pressure.
7. **Learn to use pressure**. Pressure brings everything together. Without that concentrated moment, it is not possible to hit your peak.

The best "cure" for pressure is rest. When you need it, and refuse to take it, not only are you subject to physical reprisals – ulcers, strokes and heart attacks, to name a few – but *you may be working yourself right out of a job!* There's no denying that an individual's thinking and overall productivity diminish under stress. Loss of ability can eventually result in failure to receive a promotion, actual demotion, or, in severe cases, the loss of a job.

Any reduction in work pressures is better than *no* reduction, but complete abstinence is the most curative of all. Get plenty of sleep. Shun the use of unnecessary drugs. Accept no visitors or telephone calls.

Such a period of rest gives you a chance to review your priorities. Is all the stress you have been under getting you to the place you want to be? If not, can you think of another, less stressful approach? If your previous goals are unrealistic, create some new, less stress-producing ones.

When it's time to go back to work, go at it slowly. Don't try to "make up for lost time." Avoid returning to the old, stress-inducing habits. See if you can't delegate more of your work, especially those things that have caused you the greatest stress.

Success in life is determined largely by three things: 1) how well we are understood, 2) how much we are needed and 3) how we deal with failure. Since some failure is certain, the challenge is to prepare for success while adjusting to the setbacks which are inevitable.

> There is the greatest practical benefit in making a few failures early in life.
>
> —Thomas Huxley, author

CHAPTER 8

Reaction to Rejection

> It is common sense to take a method and try it. If it fails, admit it frankly and try another. But above all, try *something*.
>
> —Franklin Delano Roosevelt,
> U.S. President

It's not difficult to recognize the obvious signs of trouble that can lead to a layoff: the company's earnings are down, budgets have been cut, business just isn't looking good. People probably will be released, and you could be one of them.

In other cases, there are more subtle signs that could indicate that your job is on the line.

- Your boss doesn't look you in the eye anymore and seems uncomfortable in your presence.
- You no longer are invited to meetings you used to attend.
- An expected pay raise or promotion does not materialize.

- You haven't had any new job assignments lately.
- Coworkers are beginning to avoid you.
- Things seem more strained at work.

Being alert to these early signals can be important. If you move quickly, perhaps you will be able to turn things around and save your job. If that isn't possible, at least you will have more time to negotiate for a more favorable separation package and get an earlier start in looking for another job.

Quiz on Handling Rejection

As a practice exercise in handling rejection, give yourself this little yes-or-no quiz.

❑Y ❑N

1. If someone says "no" to you, criticizes, or becomes angry with you, do you usually feel rejected?

❑Y ❑N

2. When rejected, do you generally feel that it's because of something you have done wrong?

❑Y ❑N

3. Whether it was the clothes you wore or the resume you sent, or perhaps a remark someone made about you, do you make sure to find out the specific reason you were rejected?

❑Y ❑N

4. If you are rejected, does it usually take you longer than twenty minutes to decide to do something about it?

❑Y ❑N

5. When you decide to do something about a rejection, do you usually have a plan to figure out the best way to overcome it?

❑Y ❑N

6. When you probe into the possible reason for rejection, do you ever think: "I actually set myself up for this?"

❑Y ❑N

7. Do you give yourself permission, now and then, to fail?

❑Y ❑N

8. Is your feeling of rejection – or the intensity of it – partly due to the fact that you're currently more vulnerable than usual or under a greater amount of pressure?

❑Y ❑N

9. Is it difficult for you to reject others, even in the most humane way possible, when they deserve it?

❑Y ❑N

10. Does rejection seem to mean more than that to you – something out of proportion to the situation?

❑Y ❑N

The proper responses should have been:

1. *No.* Anger, criticism, and refusal are not the same as rejection. People who love us frequently become angry with us; indeed, people tend to become angrier at someone with whom they are deeply involved.
2. *No.* Just as negatives from others don't necessarily mean they are rejecting you, a real rejection does not mean that you should reject yourself.
3. *Yes.* In order to know *who* is wrong, one has to know *what* is wrong.
4. *No.* The amount of time it takes you to do something is important.
5. *Yes.* Fine-tuning your ability to handle rejection – learning how to react to it, assess it, and decide to do something about it – is important.
6. *No.* Most of us do set ourselves up, subconsciously at least, for failure – and would answer this question incorrectly. Those who do recognize this fact, and handle it, would give the correct answer.
7. *Yes.* Human beings are fallible, and they *do* fail. That's all right, because you must take risks if you are to achieve success, and you *must* fail now and then. In order to fail, you must give yourself *permission* to fail.
8. *Yes.* When you do fail and are reasonably rejected, other factors frequently enter

in, so that the feeling of rejection is out of proportion to what it should be. It is important to recognize this and to identify the cause.

9. *No.* As a rule, the person who has problems in handling rejection also has problems with rejecting properly.
10. *No.* This question is a bridge toward understanding what rejection objectively *should* be and what it sometimes becomes to us: a sense of loss or failure.

> Failure is a learning experience,
> a necessary pathway to success,
> an opportunity to try something new.

Failure often tends to make the individual lose perspective – to feel that he or she alone has fallen short of success. Nothing could be more foolish. No one throughout the pages of man's long history has been free of failure.

> Not failure, but low aim, is crime.
> —James Russell Lowell, author

Everyone Loses Sometimes

The trouble is that we are conditioned to win. Losing often is traumatic. We make winning all-important. We can't accept failure.

Losing can deepen understanding – increase our appreciation for others – develop greater empathy and sympathy – produce authentic humility – soften character – mature the ego.

Winning, on the other hand, is not free of pitfalls. It can encourage arrogance – nurture impatience – stimulate contempt for losers – harden character and over-inflate the ego.

Reality is winning and losing. Prepare for reality and learn from both.

> Here is a useful idea when negotiating: Sometimes it's best to offer an item not important to you so it will seem like the other person won when you concede it.

Limit Liabilities

As difficult as it may be to believe, some people unnecessarily *create* failure situations for themselves. Some situations feed an individual's insecurity and doubt. Then they become breeding grounds for stress.

Some examples:

- You habitually accept more work than you possibly can get done.
- You create, and then don't meet, unrealistic personal deadlines.
- You must be number one in everything that you do.
- You acknowledge only what you do wrong and ignore what you do right.
- Without any evidence to that effect, you believe that you have disappointed someone important to you.
- You set, then fail to meet, perfectionist standards.
- You feel cheated and insecure every time someone else gets ahead.
- You have developed the habit of procrastinating.

> Putting off an easy thing makes it hard.
> Putting off a hard thing makes it impossible.
> —Charles Wilson, executive

As a success indicator, how well you deal with adversity is far more important than how intelligent you are, say Paul G. Stoltz author of *Adversity Quotient: Turning Obstacles into Opportunities* (Wiley & Sons Inc.) He contends that unlike IQ, which is a tattoo you tend to wear your whole life and is very difficult to change, AQ (Adversity Quotient) can be significantly improved in a very short time.

To raise your AQ you must first learn to realize whether your typical reaction to adversity is constructive or destructive. He argues that people who have a high AQ, who consistently respond to adversity in a positive way, are going to have a positive attitude. And the people who are constantly beaten down by adversity are not.

> When you won't take a risk,
> your world stands still.

The Power of Persistence

Many people who seek success have been conditioned to stop the pursuit short of their goal for one overpowering reason: fear of failing. As you change your attitude toward failure and rejection, performance can improve. To do so, follow these suggestions:

1. Accept the challenge to know yourself better so that you can develop your own potential. Determine which responsibilities or activities you tend to avoid.
2. Watch how you react to negatives. Ask: "Which is more important to me, to achieve something significant or to avoid failure?"

Resolve to handle the possibility of failure as you pursue significant performance.

3. Determine how you can eliminate obstacles that smother growth. Too often, we accept obstacles that we could have removed. Once the obstacle is removed, the path of achievement and success becomes more clear.

Success comes when we stretch further than we thought we could.

4. Understand that failure and success are both a part of the process of achieving. You must know how to feel successful, even when you are falling short of success much of the time.
5. Failure alone shouldn't really bother you. It is the rejection often associated with failure that concerns us. Learn to cope with rejection. People often are successful largely because of their ability to handle failure.

Those who criticize progress are usually substitutes who never get into the game.

Babe Ruth's strikeout record was among the highest in baseball history. He is not remembered for that, but for his home-run success. Fans of Ruth know, however, that he reacted identically to the cheers that greeted a game-winning home run and the jeers that greeted a game-losing strikeout. He'd doff his cap and wave to the crowd! Babe Ruth conditioned himself to react successfully whether he was succeeding or failing. Home run or strikeout, his reaction was the same.

Get Feedback

Some companies are beginning to evaluate employees by asking a panel of internal customers and other "stakeholders" to answer questions about their performance.

You can do this yourself by asking a couple of your internal customers for feedback on what you do well and what you need to change. Try not to stack the deck with people who are bound to be on your side. Seek a balance between your fans and those whose praise may not be quite so ardent. You may learn something!

Go through the same exercise with your co-workers. What suggestions do they have for your improvement? In companies with self-directed work teams, peer review is common. It's another reason to treat everyone honorably.

Determine Your Worth

How do you benefit your company? That's an important question – and its answer can boost your self-esteem before, during and after your performance review. Determine what you really bring to your job and your company. Don't think in terms of what you do; think in terms of the benefits your actions reap. In other words, if you are a copywriter, you don't just write copy. You help your company sell thousands of units of your product every year. If you are the executive assistant to the vice president of sales, then you're the one who helps her stay focused on achieving next year's $12 million sales goal.

Consider what you were really hired to accomplish. Have you done it? Think results, not activities – and when your review begins, *talk* results. Relate your personal performance to objectives the company wants to accomplish.

Think results, not activities.

CHAPTER 9

The Sources of Confidence

Confidence cannot be granted or bestowed. It can only be gained by facing adversity, solving problems and building on success. Those who expect to be suddenly confident are bound to be disappointed.

> Developing confidence requires a deliberate, continuous series of increasingly difficult decisions and actions.

Confidence Grows When We . . .

- **Acknowledge changes required and prepare for them.** Robert Johnson provides an outstanding example of a person who prepared for a future ignored by others. In 1980 at age 33, he started the first cable TV channel directed at African-Americans. It became the largest publicly traded company owned by an African-American, and Johnson is now one of the richest men in the U.S.

  Johnson made good connections early as a lobbyist for the cable TV industry and has capitalized, more than any other individual, on his conviction that he could establish a television medium which would respond profitably to the rapidly growing African-American middle class.

Acknowledging changes required applies directly to selling. The best sales representatives, for example, never say no. They want their customer to know that most everything is negotiable and that they are willing to work their way out of a problem with some kind of compromise.

> Losers wait for opportunities.
> Competitors create them.

Organizations with the best sales records don't count on past successes to assure their future. They realize that customers' needs are constantly changing and they must adjust and adapt to meet these needs. They *never* assume automatic renewal of past orders.

- **Improve steadily one day at a time.** Probably the greatest passer in American football before WWII was Sammy Baugh. While practicing before his first game with the Washington Redskins in 1937, his coach suggested it would be better for his receivers if he could throw the ball around their face, and he should use the eye as a target. Baugh's response was a key to his accuracy – "Which eye?" he asked.

Baugh went on to prove once and for all that the forward pass would be the key to success in professional football. Until he came along, passing was used more in desperation than as a necessity. His first pro season, he completed a then record 91 passes and led the Redskins to the NFL Championship. Friends at the time called him, "The Babe Ruth of Football."

Wilma Rudolph was diagnosed with polio when she was four years old. They said she would be paralyzed for life. But 16 years later, she became a world track champion and won 3 gold medals at the 1960 Olympics.

After doctors recommended massage therapy, Wilma's mother worked on her at home. Finally, after many months, she was able to move her toes. A few years later, she was walking with leg braces.

In her junior year at Tennessee State University, she tried out for the women's track team and in the 1960 Olympics, became the first American woman to win 3 gold medals in a single year.

- **Correct mistakes quickly.**

> It isn't what we don't know that gives us trouble, it's what we know that ain't so.
> —Will Rogers, actor and humorist

Founders of the Clorox Company started it when they pooled $100 each. They wanted a product which would be a powerful bleach for commercial use. An early investor, C.R. Murray, took home a sample to show his wife Annie. Annie saved the company by giving free samples to her customers at the store she operated with her husband. The product became very popular as a laundry aid and disinfectant and the company has never looked back on its original purpose.

The Limited, Inc. was founded by H. Leslie Wexner after he left his family's retail store. He had disagreements with his father and borrowed $5,000 from his aunt to open a small, retail women's clothing store in Columbus, Ohio. Wexner believed that his father had too much money in inventory for his formal and business clothing. He believed that casual clothes could be sold more quickly and more profitably even though the margins were less. He was right. The Limited expanded to include thousands of stores, among them brands such as Lane Bryant, Abercrombie and Fitch, Victoria's Secret, and Bath and Body Works.

- **Make goals visible.** The best way to get involvement of the people you need is to make sure everyone understands goals agreed upon, and the action plans needed to achieve them. When this happens, there is a better chance that people will exert pressure on each other to succeed. No one wants to face the embarrassment of being behind schedule or the one who did not meet the responsibility they accepted.

In addition, deadlines become more realistic when people realize that their reputation is at stake if they don't deliver what they promised.

- **Exploit opponents' weaknesses.**

> Opportunities are created when we see what others do not.

Ken Iverson was struggling to survive in his small company which manufactured steel joists and girders used in construction. He desperately needed a way to save money and determined how to recycle steel scrap using an electric arc furnace. His plan was so successful that these "mini mills" now produce more than one half of all the steel made in the U.S. His company Nucor has become the third largest steel producer in America.

Although he was only nineteen years old and a college freshman at the University of Texas, Michael Dell saw an opportunity to benefit from what major producers of personal computers overlooked. Unencumbered by any kind of bureaucracy or permission requirements, he began to buy surplus PCs and increase their capability. He bypassed dealers and sold his machines directly via the phone and regular mail. Soon he was selling $80,000 worth of computers a month, still operating out of his college dorm room. Michael Dell's company became the world leader it is today because he capitalized on opportunities the giant companies overlooked or were unwilling to try.

- **Are authentic and do not create artificial situations or relationships.**

> To detect winners, look for confidence when under stress.

Bernard Kerik's life has been an endless series of overcoming obstacles. His mother was an alcoholic and a prostitute. His father divorced his mother and moved into a tough neighborhood. His mother was murdered when he was only four. His earliest memories involve living on the edge of the law. By age 15, he was urged to drop out of high school because he missed 35 straight days.

Kerik drifted until he enlisted in the Army, where he became an expert at training sentry dogs. At age 30, he began as a trainee at the New York Police Academy, and eventually became the head of Riker's Island, New York's famous jail complex. His work there attracted the attention of Rudolph Giuliani, then the U.S. attorney who planned to run for mayor of New York City. When elected, Giuliani selected Kerik as Police Commissioner, where he led in the reduction of crime by 12%. Nationwide recognition came when he coordinated the rescue of tens of thousands of people in the World Trade Center on September 11, 2001.

- **Encourage and reward new solutions.** Perhaps no enterprise in the world has benefited as much from its creative employees as Nokia, a 137-year old Scandinavian company with annual sales of over $31 billion, operating in 130 countries. The acknowledged leader in the mobile phone industry, Nokia sells five phones every second. Its 38% market share is greater than its nearest 3 rivals combined.

  Most experts agree that Nokia's leadership is based upon the way it builds innovation into its daily operations. Work groups are empowered to make their ideas happen. Independent profit centers have the autonomy to do their own research, development and marketing. The company's R&D budget is $3 billion and 40% of its 52,000 employees are involved in R&D.

Confidence enables us to go beyond what we know for certain.

- **Prove we deserve support.** The last time coach Bob Ladouceur's De La Salle high school football team lost a game was on December 7, 1991. Since then, they have had 11 straight unbeaten seasons with a record of 138 victories and 0 defeats. When asked to account for such a unique record, Ladouceur points to some very simple conclusions. 1) He believes that he must always be honest with his players. "If you're not who you say you are, the kids will find out quickly," he says. 2) He wants players to understand that his authority is based not on threats, but his genuine interest in them and their success. 3) When this happens, players will learn to "self-correct" during games. They will think about what they are doing wrong and make the adjustments needed.

In effect, Ladouceur is teaching his players that if he deserves their respect and they respect themselves, they will have success in their common goal, which is winning football games together. His conviction works and the team's success for such a long time is the proof.

Untapped Sources of Help

A quick way to assess career progress more objectively is to make sure that the people closest to you really understand what your job involves and how you feel about it.

One of the major but neglected causes of marital problems and career dissatisfaction is the fact the very few people really understand what their husband or wife does at work. Except for professional athletes (whose mistakes are seen on TV by millions), some national level politicians, a few "high exposure" corporate executives and spouse teams in family enterprises, most work problems (or successes) are not understood or shared at home. I use the word "share" not in the sense of talking about frustrations or complaining about certain people or circumstances, but in terms of in-depth and continuous acknowledgment of what is happening at work, how it is happening and why.

Three Steps Needed

1. The first step is open and continuing discussion. This implies a definition of love which includes a never-ending curiosity about whatever is affecting the work life of a marriage partner.
2. The second step is satisfying that curiosity by regular, firsthand knowledge of their work. How many wives or husbands do you know who regularly visit their spouse's work place to:
   - See what they do
   - Meet their boss and associates
   - Observe problems
   - Take satisfaction in successes
3. The third step is to avoid "locking out" your mate because you think he or she won't understand or doesn't have adequate background or experience to appreciate your situation. Background and experience are not necessary when the subject is your career. The only vital ingredients are a willingness to listen, to observe, to ask questions and to be empathetic. If you do these things, you will be amazed at

how little time it takes to become quite knowledgeable in your spouse's field. Not an expert, mind you, but smart enough to be helpful, and that's all that is needed.

Look Inside First

My work with executives and owners over the years has convinced me that American businesses are far better off working to maximize the contributions of their *existing* employees than constantly searching for outsiders. Seeking and training new people is an important responsibility, but it's also costly and time-consuming. New talent is clearly required to account for normal attrition, and to accommodate growth, but there should be no need to bring in an "outsider" for a key position if you can locate a suitable candidate within the company. This means that every individual can have an excellent opportunity for further advancement *if they* continue to demonstrate the capability to perform better than newcomers.

Confidence Targets

- **Look for changes needed.**
- **Correct mistakes quickly.**
- **Improve steadily.**
- **Make goals stretching.**
- **Try new solutions.**
- **Use failure to your advantage.**
- **Deserve support.**

CHAPTER 10

Failure Is Not Fatal

The people who framed our Declaration of Independence granted us certain inalienable rights: life, liberty, and the *pursuit* of happiness. They said we had the right to *pursue* it, but nobody ever gave us any assurance that we would always be able to *capture* it.

The formula for failure is clear: Never accept responsibility.

When Naomi Judd was seventeen, she got pregnant and married her boyfriend. Five years later she found herself living two thousand miles from home with two kids to support, no husband, and no job. Without a car, she found a minimum-wage job as a receptionist within walking distance of her apartment. She did things no one else wanted to do and was soon promoted. She quickly learned she was more capable than she thought, and has proven it many times since. This is the same Naomi Judd who has won six Grammy Awards and sold over twenty million country music albums.

> **Show me the one who has overcome the most difficulties and I'll know who to bet on.**

Setback vs. Failure

Failure doesn't result from the lack of achievement; it comes from the lack of *trying*. This is not to say that the pathway to success is without hazards. Disillusionment lurks around every corner. But those who aspire to success must learn how to face failure, how to deal with it, and how to go on with the more positive aspects of their careers.

It helps to learn the difference between a setback and a failure. Failure is destructive. A setback can be overcome. It can be instructive. It can be constructive. It can be character building. People who suffer a setback pick themselves up, regroup, and try again. Those who believe they are failures give up.

> Failure is not the enemy of success.
> It is the soil in which it grows.

The trick is to overcome the feeling of loss as quickly as possible and replace it with a positive experience. Successful people bounce back because they believe that next time they will succeed. No matter how bleak things look, they maintain an optimistic inner spirit that helps them surmount obstacles. To them, defeat is merely a temporary setback.

Until Cyrus McCormick came along at age 22, grain had been harvested for centuries throughout the world in a backbreaking way, using a long, curved knife blade called a scythe. McCormick decided that the job could be done mechanically and worked hard in his family's blacksmith shop before developing a "reciprocating blade" that moved back and forth as it cut the grain. This reaper became successful and could do the same amount of work that 24 people with scythes could do in a day.

Eventually McCormick built a factory in Chicago, so that he could serve the rapidly growing markets in the middle-west. Employment there was one of the biggest factors in Chicago's rapid growth. But McCormick didn't stop there – he locked in his customers by including a written guarantee with each reaper and sold them at a fixed price so that his dealers did not have to haggle with customers over each sale. McCormick's determination to overcome the obstacles where others had failed for centuries enabled him to sell 250,000 machines by 1885. His company later became International Harvester.

Nathan Cummings was known as an eternal optimist. He kept a plaque in his office which read, "Nothing will be accomplished if all possible objections must first be overcome." That outlook enabled him to systematically acquire companies which ultimately became Consolidated Foods, a food processing, distribution and retailing giant, which was later renamed Sara Lee Corp.

Early in his career, Cummings went broke trying to operate a small shoemaking business. He referred to that time as "the greatest thing to happen to me," because it served as an incentive to concentrate his energies in new areas with greater potential.

Cummings outlook toward defeat has been a model for many other successful businesses. He was quick to cut his losses by dropping poor performing companies. And he spent little time agonizing about his setbacks in business.

> Failure is caused more by a lack of perspiration than inspiration.

Most of the time, when progress is not what we want it to be, we have allowed daily pressures to keep holding us back. At best we are stalled and at worst we are going backwards.

How to Determine Your Pressure Quotient (P.Q.)

Here is a way to determine your pressure points. Do you:

1. Finish others' sentences before they do?

   ❑Y ❑N
2. Move, walk or eat rapidly?

   ❑Y ❑N
3. Prefer summaries instead of perusing the total document?

   ❑Y ❑N

4. Become easily angered in slow lines or traffic?

❑Y ❑N

5. Generally feel impatient?

❑Y ❑N

6. Find yourself unaware of details?

❑Y ❑N

7. Do two or more things simultaneously?

❑Y ❑N

8. Feel guilty if you relax or vacation?

❑Y ❑N

9. Evaluate your worth quantitatively, using tangibles like your salary, athletic game scores, number of employees, or grades as a measure?

❑Y ❑N

10. Schedule more and more activities into less and less time?

❑Y ❑N

11. Think about other things while talking to someone?

❑Y ❑N

12. Exhibit nervous gestures (grinding your teeth, clenching your fists, or drumming your fingers)?

❑Y ❑N

13. Continue to assume more and more responsibility?

❑Y ❑N

continued

14. Explosively accentuate "key" words in ordinary speech when there is no reason to do so?

❑Y ❑N

15. Work hurriedly even through the deadline is not pressing?

❑Y ❑N

If you answered "yes" to 10 or more of these questions, then claim your "A," for "Type A" behavior. This is one of the few times when an "A" can lead to an "F" – for failure. As in heart failure, "Type A" personalities typically are more prone to stress. As a result, they run a higher risk of heart attack, "Type B" people, those who exhibit the opposite of the above 15 points, are far less likely to have heart problems stemming from stress. In fact, "Type A" people tend to have twice the rate of heart disease as their "B" colleagues.

The four central causes of pressure are: change, unpredictability, lack of control, and conflict. Recognition, prevention, and pacing are the keys to coping effectively with it. The need is to recognize both internal and external causes of pressure. Recurrence can be prevented by searching for solutions and adopting healthy alternatives, accompanied by adequate rest, relaxation and exercise.

If you believe hard times
can crush you – they will.

Are You in a Pressure Cooker?

Any of the following decisions can help decrease pressure.

- **Don't stay in limbo**. Doubts multiply with delay. Make a choice and get on with it.
- **Balance addition with subtraction**. Resist the temptation to become overloaded, and drop lowest ranking chores.
- **Set realistic deadlines**. Give yourself an acceptable range of time for completion, not a single set date. Allow time to adjust to changes. Increase your contact with people who will provide support.
- **Seek assignments** which will capitalize on your strengths and minimize the impact of your weaknesses.

Why Good People Burn Out

Very often when individuals and work groups accomplish much less than their potential it is not because of bad hiring decision, misfits, or people who should be fired, but because formerly good employees have "burned out" and no longer contribute according to their ability. Often the major reasons for these situations are related to unresolved pressure. Everyone has his or her own capacity for stress or pressure. What we all need, however, is a reliable means to:

- Identify the sources for pressure which are most likely to affect us.
- Develop mechanisms for coping with them.
- Know when it's over.

The tribal wisdom of the Lakota Indians, passed on from generation to generation, says: "When you discover that you are riding a dead horse, the best strategy is to dismount." Too often however, employers (especially government agencies) use strange "strategies" to deal with this problem. Do any of these sound familiar?

- Buy a stronger whip.
- Change riders.
- Appoint a committee to study the horse.
- Arrange visits to see how other companies ride dead horses.
- Lower standards so that dead horses can be included.
- Reclassify the dead horse as living-impaired.
- Hire outside contractors to ride the dead horse.
- Harness several dead horses together to increase speed.
- Provide additional funding and/or training to increase dead horse's performance.

- Do a productivity study to see if lighter riders would improve the dead horse's performance.
- Declare that since the dead horse does not have to be fed, it is less costly and carries lower overhead. Therefore, it contributes substantially more to the bottom line of the economy than do some other horses.
- Rewrite the expected performance requirements for all horses.

Is it any wonder that good people who must carry the load in these organizations sometimes burn out?

> All roads to success are paved with some mistakes.

Change Brings New Tensions

A change of any kind challenges our sense of adequacy. That's what usually happens when a business changes hands, particularly in these days of fast-moving mergers, acquisitions and downsizing. Pressure becomes an ever-present fact of life for many who once felt secure in their jobs, and confident about the future.

By losing independence, management at nearly every acquired company also loses stature. Executives used to calling the shots start reporting to a layer of management above them. A number inevitably are dismissed because the parent company doesn't need two people for every corporate slot.

If this were not stressful enough, consider the signals from new bosses indicating changes will be made. Criticism of past management practices and results is not likely to calm jittery nerves. Many will be told to move on. Others will be asked to retire, and some will simply quit to avoid being fired. Others can anticipate demotion, or a sharp curtailment of their authority.

There is no doubt about it: job pressure can erode efficiency, productivity, and even mental and physical health.

Getting Rid of Pressure

When people suffer burnout, it is usually because they either have too much to do or they don't know exactly what to do. These problems can often be reduced or eliminated if we:

Walk away. It is often advantageous to walk away from the pressure source for a short period of time.

Ventilate. A person under pressure will usually feel better just by having someone listen to their concerns.

Take short naps. When possible, a 15 to 20 minute nap may provide the tension release needed.

Relieve anger. Unexpressed anger and hostility can cause pressure which can be relieved via exercising.

Act. Procrastination increases guilt feelings. Just getting started on a postponed project can be enough to energize instead of immobilize.

Use professional counseling. When fear of reprisals or loss of self-esteem is at issue, counseling may be a viable alternative. The individual is then free to express fears, anxieties, and concerns within the confines of a professional's office.

Who do you work with who could benefit from one or more of these suggestions? Jot the name beside each of the italicized headings above. Could you benefit? Which alternative are you willing to try? When?

Case: Who or What to Blame?

Consider this case involving several different reactions to pressure. Jim Roberts, claims branch manager, supervises four section chiefs, each of whom manages the work of twenty claims clerks. They process claims, initiated by policyholders through local company "reps". The work is mainly a mechanical processing of cases and requires average intelligence and a high school education.

JIM: I've called this meeting to get to the heart of a problem we've simply got to lick. Top management hit me again on the increasing number of complaints the company has been getting from policyholders about disposition of claims. For example, the latest is a policyholder in Nebraska whose claim was denied. On appeal, a clear-cut clerical error was discovered. The policyholder was right. We looked bad and mistreated our policyholder. The frequency of these errors has increased over the past year. We simply have to improve our accuracy.

MARY: Frankly, Jim, I'm glad you called this meeting. I've *seen* the increase of mistakes in my own section. And I can't see anything I can do about it. These clerks are simply not being trained properly. They come to me with loads of general ideas but we have to give them *experience* and, while they are getting it, mistakes pile up – and many aren't caught.

MARK: I have to agree with Mary. The recruiting people are really scraping the bottom of the barrel. I can't prove it, but I know the people I'm getting this past year are at a lower intelligence level.

AL: That's right, Jim. We're getting the best we can from these clods but the results are poor. The real trouble is getting them to put out a little effort and make their quota. Most of them are slow-down types – very little drive. They just don't make quota.

MARK: Well, Al, you know we have a morale problem that is, in my opinion, the real problem we're talking about at this meeting. And – no offense, but I don't think an attitude like yours helps morale much. Workers sense disrespect and resent it. If you could get morale up . . .

JIM: Well, let's not argue leadership styles. I think we all agree we've had a morale problem – last year's high turnover shows that – but I don't think morale is that bad. We simply have to insist on more attention to accuracy. That's the problem.

PETE: I've said this before in meetings but I can't help insisting that the real cause of all our trouble is the crazy system of forms our clerks use. They haven't been revised in 10 years. If we could get support upstairs for the revisions I suggested, Jim . . .

AL: Right, Pete, I like your drafts. They're foolproof. Why can't we get action upstairs? I often think that's our problem – no communication between policy and operational levels.

MARK: All we need is another *change*! Like the company, moving to the suburbs last year. My people pestered me every day until that was decided. Our key problem is that we have *too much change.*

The meeting continued in this pattern for about two hours. No decisions were made and most left the meeting feeling it was a waste of time and nothing was accomplished.

1. Who in this case is exhibiting pressure?

   How?

2. Make some suggestions for reducing the pressure you've described.

3. The company president has asked you to help Jim Roberts. In priority order, what would your first three recommendations be?

   A. Recommendation:

      Reason?

      Need to be met?

      Benefits?

B. Recommendation:

Reason?

Need to be met?

Benefits?

C. Recommendation:

Reason?

Need to be met?

Benefits?

Reducing the frequency and impact of burnout requires more than good intentions. Causes and cures must be identified realistically. By starting with the recommendations in this section, you will begin to understand your needs more specifically and see how you can be helpful to others when effectiveness declines.

For Example:

"Heeeeeeeeeeeeeeeere's Johnny!"

Ed McMahon discovered at an early age that he had an ability to sell. He also quickly discovered that rejection is as much a part of selling as are customers. How does this pro handle such situations? The biggest challenge, he believes, is to learn how to take the sting out of rejection. It is possible to secure a huge success, then experience a series of depressing failures. Men and women who sell for a living know they're going to be turned down. That's the nature of the work: You can't be a successful salesperson without losing some sales.

Fortitude is gained only through hardship. Endurance grows only by enduring.

CHAPTER 11

Sharing the Load

Leaders collect keys they use to unlock potential in themselves and others.

The ultimate goal of organizations is to achieve desired results in a climate in which people are *self-motivated.* To get to that point requires an understanding of some fundamental principles. This chapter is devoted to those principles. In it you will be involved in a variety of experiences, from analyzing a case featuring a negatively motivated employee to testing a formula for success.

Your first assignment is to carefully read the case "Loyalty or Sabotage," which follows. Make notes in the margin as you read. You may also want to underline or highlight key points. Next, answer the three questions which follow the case. Use key words only. Be brief. At your earliest convenience discuss the case with someone else to see where you agree or disagree, and why. For example, Rick certainly got off to a bad start with Courtney by not seeking her input at their first meeting. How would you have dealt with her at that point?

Loyalty or Sabotage?

Rick Jordan, head of Purchasing at the Freeport Center, flinched a little as he heard the angry voice of Larry Wyman, the Center's Distribution Manager, over the phone. "What's going on, Rick? We're almost completely out of storage racks. I ordered a supply over a month ago, and I still haven't received or heard anything about the order."

"I'm really sorry, Larry. I'll check on it right away."

Rick put down the receiver, frowned, then pressed the buzzer on his desk. "Jennie, would you please ask Courtney Stone to come in?"

Rick had come to Freeport only a few months before having set an impressive record as purchasing manager at a nearby company. Nevertheless, he was positive that he knew the name of the person responsible for the mistake: Courtney Stone.

Courtney had been at Freeport for a number of years, most of them spent in the purchasing department. She was bright, talented, and very popular with her co-workers. Her former supervisor, an easy-going man who had recently retired, had been impressed with Courtney and had given her quite a bit of responsibility. Although Courtney was younger than most of the people in the department, Rick had observed that the importance of her duties never caused her to act in a condescending manner toward her older co-workers. Courtney was always more than willing to take on additional tasks if there was a lull in her workday or if someone was sick or on vacation.

Although supervisors in many other departments had nothing but good things to say about her, Rick had begun to think differently about Courtney's character and ability. Shortly after taking over, he had called all of his staff together and outlined some changes he wanted to see implemented immediately. Quite disturbed about them, Courtney had exclaimed, "But the way we've been doing things for the past few years has always worked out fine. Why change?"

"Well, I think there's always room for improvement in even the best departments," Rick had replied. "I'm sure you'll agree with me after a few months, and I hope you will give me your best cooperation right now."

After that, Courtney never said a word about the changes. She seemed eager to please and followed instructions to the letter. And that was precisely the problem, Rick thought.

Rick went over in his mind the first time such an incident with Courtney occurred. A shipment of inventory control forms had not arrived on time, and the department had undergone a somewhat frantic search before its arrival to find out what had happened to it. When Rick telephoned the supplier, he was told that the company had received the order a few weeks late because it had been sent to the old address. "Didn't you give your people that information?" the clerk on the other end of the line had asked Rick. "Of course I did," Rick said, wondering what had caused the delay.

Later on, when he questioned Courtney, she explained, "I was just following instructions, Rick. You didn't say that the supplier had a new address." Rick was positive that she had known about it. He asked a few employees about it, and they all said that they indeed had been informed of the change of address. Rick was sure that he hadn't overlooked Courtney, but he couldn't prove it. And he couldn't fire or suspend her for obeying orders.

The sound of footsteps broke Rick's train of thought. He tried to control his temper as he asked her about the missing storage rack.

Courtney smiled and said, "You told me that an order requesting a change in brand required your approval. Distribution requested a change in suppliers. I put the order on your desk in one of those piles. Didn't you see it?"

As Courtney stepped back, obviously enjoying the situation, Rick took a pile and began to rummage through it. Then he stopped, looked at Courtney, and began to tremble with rage. She knew very well, he thought, what the procedure was for getting an order approved. She should have given it to Jennie, his secretary, so that it would come to his attention immediately.

What would you do?

1. How should Rick deal with Courtney now?

2. Was this situation inevitable – or could Rick have prevented it?

3. Can Rick do anything to change Courtney's attitude toward him and the job?

Unlocking Potential

To extend what we alone can do, we must delegate.

In my consulting work I frequently ask clients who say they are overloaded, "Why don't you give some of this to someone else?" The answer typically is, "No one else is capable of handling it now." That's the dilemma of poor leaders – by failing to provide experiences for people to grow, they prohibit them from learning to handle increased responsibility.

In this chapter you will be asked in a variety of ways to make decisions about how to share your load effectively.

How Much Delegating Is Enough?

Here is a simple way to find out how much delegating is enough. Answer each question honestly.

1. Do you often work overtime?

❑Yes ❑No

2. Do you take work home evenings and on weekends?

❑Yes ❑No

3. Is your unfinished work increasing?

❑Yes ❑No

4. Are daily operations so time-consuming that you have little time left for planning and other important matters?

❑Yes ❑No

5. Do you personally supervise or perform all details to have a job done right?

❑Yes ❑No

6. Do you frequently have to postpone long-range projects?

❑Yes ❑No

7. Are you harassed by constant unexpected emergencies?

❑Yes ❑No

8. Do you lack confidence in others' abilities to shoulder more responsibility?

❑Yes ❑No

9. Do you find yourself irritable and complaining when the work of your group doesn't meet your expectations?

❑Yes ❑No

10. Do people defer most decisions to you?

❑Yes ❑No

11. Do you instruct people to perform certain activities, rather than to accomplish certain goals?

❑Yes ❑No

12. Have people stopped presenting their ideas to you?

❑Yes ❑No

13. Do operations slow down much when you are away?

❑Yes ❑No

14. Do you feel that you're abdicating your role as leader if you ask for assistance?

❑Yes ❑No

15. Do you believe that your status and compensation automatically mean that you have to be overworked?

❑Yes ❑No

If the majority of your answers are affirmative, it's likely that you're not delegating enough.

Take careful notice of the number of responsibilities you would retain for yourself. *Is it realistic?*

Dell Computer Corp. is a good example of a very successful company which pushes responsibility for customer satisfaction down to the individual employee. Because salespeople are the single point of accountability, it has been possible for Dell to eliminate the tremendous cost of having a large, expensive inventory and to build only what is ordered by the customer. The same salesperson works with that customer until delivery.

Retailer Nordstrom started as a shoe store in Seattle in 1901, and now has over 140 stores in 27 states with 42,000 employees. Its enviable reputation is based on a simple creed, "satisfy the customer." Front line employees need and get top management support with authority to decide on price adjustments, returns or specific problems.

If a salesperson's commissions don't reach a target, they get the hourly rate. If the target is met or exceeded they get more. The performers lead meetings and share their experiences. Those who don't reach targets get special help. The system tends to be self-correcting. Those who don't like the competitive atmosphere drop out.

Gibson – The Ultimate Delegator

Let's look at the case of a man with very strong convictions on this subject. Gibson was "discovered" by a consultant who was in the process of interviewing managers in a client organization. The consultant was trying to find out whether people were offered the opportunity to initiate discussion and actively participate in the decision-making process or were merely afforded the opportunity to hear about decisions the boss had made.

When asked about meetings with team members, Gibson said he met with them regularly on the same day each week for two hours, "so they can tell me about the decisions they've made." His exact words were, "I don't make their decisions for them and I don't believe in participating in the decisions they should be making either. We hold the weekly meeting so that I can keep informed on how they're doing."

When a team member was asked if Gibson made decisions, he answered, "No, he doesn't. Everything he told you is true. He decided not to get involved in decisions that we are being paid to make, so he stopped making them. They tell me he has been promoted twice since he adopted this approach."

When asked if he had ever tried to get Gibson to make a decision for him, the response was: "Only once. I had been on the job for only about a week when I ran into an operating problem I couldn't solve, so I phoned Gibson. He answered the phone and I told him who I was and that I had a problem. His response was instantaneous: 'Fine, solving problems is what you are being paid for.' When I persisted, he was sharp and suggested that I ask one of the other men to help me with my problem. I didn't know which one to consult and insisted on seeing him. Gibson finally agreed to see me right away. He asked me what my *problem* was and wrote down my answers. He asked what the *conditions* for its *solution* were, and I replied that I didn't understand what he meant. He said, 'If you don't know what conditions have to be satisfied for a solution to be reached, how do you know when you've solved the problem?' He told me he would work out this problem with me *this* time only, but that it was *my* job."

When asked about the weekly meetings, another person said, "We all sit around that big table in Gibson's office talking about the decisions we've made, and, if we got help, who helped us. Participants make comments – especially if the particular decision being discussed was like one they had to make themselves at some point or if it had some direct effect on their own job." She said Gibson talked very little at most meetings, but did pass on new developments he had heard about from the main office.

The organization's CEO confirmed that Gibson managed the best department but had a high turnover rate. The reason he said was, "Most of the people go on to be managers themselves. Because of Gibson, they are used to taking responsibility."

At another meeting Gibson was asked about the individual who takes over the weekly meeting when he is gone, and how he chooses the person to fill that slot. "That's simple," he said. "I pick the person most often referred to for help in dealing with problems. Then I try him/her out in this assignment while I'm off. It's good training. Those who can handle it I recommend for any vacancies that come along at the manager level. The main-office people always contact me for candidates."

All managers interviewed, except Gibson, either stated explicitly or made it clear during the course of the interviews that they themselves made the important decisions in their meetings. They received suggestions, considered their sources, and then made the final decision. In using Gibson's approach, they made it obvious they believed one of the key responsibilities of an upper-level executive is to act as chief decision-maker. They *believed* it was a joint decision, but people themselves thought they were manipulated and avoided taking risks. Gibson did allow some margin in case emergency action on his part was inevitable, but made it clear he wanted to hear about problems after they had been solved and about decisions after they had been made.

Bottom line: Gibson's overriding concern was with **results** achieved either via methods people developed themselves or by working with their peers. He refused to do their work for them, even at the risk of incurring short-term costs. He put his time and energy into negotiating objectives, adapting to changing conditions, allocating resources for present and future effectiveness, and recruiting people ready for self-development.

1. Would you want Gibson as your boss? Why? Why not? List advantages and disadvantages:

   Advantages — Disadvantages

2. Would Gibson be a successful manager in your organization? Why? Why Not?

> **The best leaders teach people how to "self-correct."**

Delegation Quiz

Answer each of these questions honestly, based on this scale:

Definite Weakness	1 – 2
Rarely Effective	3 – 4
Average Performance	5 – 6
Usually Effective	7 – 8
Definite Strength	9 – 10

1. Our team members understand our objectives and know what is to be done, when, how well, and by whom.

   _____

2. I know which of my responsibilities I must meet myself and which I can delegate.

   _____

3. I encourage initiative in our team members.

   _____

4. I delegate the final decision often enough.

   _____

5. I avoid doing the work of team members.

   _____

6. I show genuine interest in the work we are doing.

   _____

7. I am confident team members can handle the work I give them.

   _____

8. I give the guidance, training, and authority needed to make decisions without me.

    _____

9. I regularly assess the quality of my work and that of our team.

    _____

10. I use delegation to help team members gain new skills and grow in the organization.

    _____

TOTAL

If your score is over 75, you are delegating well.
If it is between 50 and 75, your delegation is acceptable, but could improve.
If it under 50, you should begin immediately to concentrate on improving your delegation skills.

Now ask your boss and team members to rate you in each of these areas and compare your scores with theirs. Concentrate on improving in the areas where there is disagreement.

Conclusion

The essence of leadership is to achieve results through others. Only those who learn to delegate are able to expand beyond their own ability.

Demotivate or Activate?

You have received some clues about motivation in the "Loyalty or Sabotage" case. Now it's up to you! Will you choose to "Demotivate" or "Activate?"

People are "demotivated" when you:

1. Fail to give them your undivided attention.
2. Fail to acknowledge their personal preferences.
3. Belittle their accomplishments.
4. Criticize them in front of others.
5. Are insensitive to time schedules.
6. Waiver in making a decision.
7. Do not complete your part of the work.
8. Are preoccupied with your own projects.
9. Show favoritism.

People are "activated" when you:

1. Challenge them with important work.
2. Provide necessary support services.
3. Let them know what is expected.
4. Recognize their accomplishments *appropriately*.
5. Keep them informed of changes that may affect them.
6. Go out of your way to help them.
7. Communicate progress regularly.
8. Face up to needed changes and assignments.
9. Seek their advice sincerely.
10. Demonstrate confidence in them.
11. Encourage ingenuity.

Resenting successful people is the first step to failure.

CHAPTER 12

The Team Approach to Solving Problems

The most valuable people in any organization are the problem solvers. If you don't have them, you have two choices: 1) solve problems yourself or 2) trust outsiders. Neither offers the multiple advantages and benefits of involving people who believe they have a personal stake in your success.

Organizations, like individuals, grow by solving problems. People who go through setbacks and emerge intact have gained an enormous advantage in their lives. A sense of triumph and self-esteem comes with solving difficult problems in a way no other experience provides. Problems offer the chance to display initiative, creativity and leadership.

The Value of Being a Successful Problem Solver

Unfortunately, rational problem-solving is seriously obstructed by the belief that emotional content must be eliminated first. At the time a problem is uncovered or erupts, most people have a compulsion to plunge into emotional responses of rage, fear or panic. Successful organizations recognize this hazard by concentrating on these three basic elements:

1. **Be reasonable.** Begin with an orderly, rational and constructive approach to dealing with problems.
2. **Handle emotional responses face to face.** Guessing about meaning or intent is dangerous at best.
3. **Turn every problem into an objective.** The key to being systematic and rational is to convert every problem into an objective. Starting with a grasp of all available facts, define an objective. This is the condition which would exist if the problem were resolved. Objectives can create a will to achieve as well as a path to success.

A man's car stalled in the middle of a busy street. The woman behind him honked continuously as he tried to start it. Finally, he got out and walked over to her. Smiling politely, he said, "I can't seem to get my car started, but if you'll go and start it for me, I'll stay here and lean on your horn."

Why Problems Aren't Solved

Too many problems remain long after they should have been worked through. Here are some of the most common reasons:

- Fear of criticizing supervisors.
- People tend to be protective of their positions, reputation and hopes for advancement.
- The presence of people with special expertise tends to intimidate those who are afraid of admitting ignorance.
- A sense of urgency tends to stimulate unreliable judgments.
- Personal conflicts often work against constructive, cooperative effort.
- People see problems from their own viewpoint, rather than from a broader organizational perspective.
- Focusing on a distasteful situation often clouds the atmosphere with tension, fear, and uncertainty.

These barriers must be overcome in order to develop new and better solutions. Which ones apply to you? Can you identify any of the reasons?

When Steve Odland took over as CEO of Auto Zone in early 2001, his first impression was that everyone seemed to be waiting for him to tell them what to do. His first act was to have new business cards made for the top 40 people. The title on every one of them was CEO.

Soon everyone was contributing to solving the worst problems. He calls his management style "enrolling" with a "coaching mentality." He makes sure he listens to people who deal directly with customers. He concentrates on facts and does not rush to judgment. His methods of involving as many of Auto Zone's 45,000 employees as possible in solving problems is paying off – the stock price tripled in 2002.

Problem-Solving Steps

The following steps will show you how to separate, identify, and work through a problem. Use them to fill out the Problem-Solving Worksheet on the following pages. Before you begin, take time to read the sample which appears on the following pages. Then use these steps to solve a problem of your own.

1. **Make a brief statement of the problem**. This should be no longer than two sentences. For example, "I am dissatisfied with the current level of ." Take only five minutes to do this.
2. **What is the present unsatisfactory level?** Perhaps the status or measure – of the condition in question. Find the facts.
3. **What would be a reasonable desired level?** What would be acceptable performance?

4. **How did you arrive at the estimate of desired level?** (Industry norms, professional standards, previous achievement). Be realistic.
5. **What are some of the possible causes** contributing to this unsatisfactory level of operation? (Brainstorm – come up with a long list).
6. **Of those causes**, which ones are the *most likely*?
7. **What are some of the alternative solutions or proposed courses of action?** (Brainstorm again – list ideas without evaluating).
   a. **Decide on appropriate criteria** for evaluating your alternative solutions. For example:
   b. **Contribution to objective.** How much will this course of action contribute to arriving at the desired level?
   c. **Cost** Net impact on financial position after costs are balanced by improvement.
   d. **Feasibility** – physical ability to implement the course of action, considering company policy, budgets or other restrictions.
   e. **Ideal situation** – Using the ratings of High (H), Medium (M), and Low (L), come up with an ideal score for each criterion. For example, the ideal score on the Problem-Solving Example (next page) would be High on *Contribution to Objectives,* Low in *Cost,* and High in *Feasibility.* If you prefer, substitute a

number ranking (1-10), actual dollar costs, or exact time.

f. **Score** each option or possible alternative.

8. **Based on your scores,** which alternative (or combination of alternatives) is *most likely to solve the problem*?
9. **Write out a time and action plan** using your chosen solution(s). Add target dates for beginning, completing, and evaluating the action. Include specifics and various steps or phases. This is your commitment to solving the problem. As time passes, if your evaluation indicates that there is still a problem, begin again with another group of people.

Problem Solving Example

Work through your problem by following steps A through I below.

A. **Statement of Problem** *I am dissatisfied with the current level of retail receivables in our division.*

B. **Present Level** *47 days of sales outstanding.*

C. **Reasonable Desired Level** *42-40 days of sales outstanding.*

D. **Basis for Estimate of Desired Level** *Previous historical data.*

E. **Possible Causes**

- *Attitude of retail manager – considers it low priority.*

- *Lacks knowledge of tools to handle this area.*
- *Systems flow problems.*
- *Location and size of operation.*
- *Inadequate Staff.*
- *Administers policies inconsistently.*

F. **Most Likely Causes**

- *Attitude of Retail manager – considers it low priority.*
- *Systems flow problems.*

G. **Alternative Solutions, Criteria for Evaluating**

	Contribution	Cost	Feasibility
Ideal Score	H	L	H
1. Increase staff	H	H	H
2. Take management course	M	L	H
3. Train manager in the importance of profit (and cash flow)	M	L	H
4. Dollar incentives	M	H	L
5. Communications	H	L	H
6. Organize his operation	L	L	H
7. Team to study systems	M	L	H
8. Data processing output	H	H	H
9. Clerical load reduced	M	L	H
10. Reduce approvals	H	H	H
11. Service Bureau (vs. in-house)	H	H	H
12. Improved controls	H	L	H

H. **Numbers of Above Solutions Most Nearly Meeting the Goal** *12, 5, 2, 3, 9.*

I. **Time and Action Plan: *Who* will do *What* by *When***
(Indicate for each solution listed in G.)
12) *Adopt control system used in Garden Division within 90 days. (Roy Jones)*
5) *Include article on receivables in each monthly edition of dealer magazine for next 12 months. (Linda Smith)*
2) *Send the worst offenders to appropriate management course within three months. (Each department head will decide.)*
3) *Bring in new receivables manager from Garden Division within 30 days. (Roy Jones)*
9) *Add another clerical position in the department immediately. Review when new system becomes operative. (John Polk)*

Problem-Solving Worksheet

A. **Statement of Problem**

B. **Present Level**

C. **Reasonable Desired Level**

D. **Basis for Estimate of Desired Level**

E. **Possible Causes**

F. **Most Likely Causes**

G. Alternative Solutions, Criteria for Evaluating

	Contribution	Cost	Feasibility
Ideal Score			
1			
2			
3			
4			
5			
6			
7			
8			
9			
10			

H. **Numbers of Above Solutions Most Nearly Meeting the Goal**

I. **Time and Action Plan: *Who* will do *What* by *When***
(Indicate for each solution listed in G.)

Conclusion

The ability to solve problems *before* they become disasters is a real *inside advantage.* The skills are neither complex nor mysterious. We must:

- Concentrate on high-priority needs, not trivia.
- Get the people involved who have the greatest stake in the outcome or in solving the problem.
- Concentrate on objectivity, not opinions or premature judgment.
- Seek solutions, not blame.
- Learn to use an organized systematic approach such as the one you have worked with in this chapter.

Even Stars Need Team Help

Scaling the highest peak in the world was only a dream until 1953. Who accomplished it? An unknown, unlikely son of a beekeeper from Auckland, New Zealand. Always thinking ahead, young Edmund Hillary saved the money his dad gave him to ride a school bus and ran the 5 miles each way.

After serving in the Royal New Zealand Air Force, he teamed with several experienced mountain climbers in his home country and Europe. When he decided to attempt Mt. Everest, he chose Sherpa Tenzing Norgay as his teammate. His attention to detail paid off. By collecting half-empty oxygen bottles on the ascent, they had enough to return when the bottles they had filled were empty.

The best competitors find ways to make good decisions when information is not complete and answers are not obvious.

Oscar Robertson was voted the *Player of the Century* by the *National Association of Basketball Coaches* in 2000. His approach to life and career is simple – "the Lord will give you more if you take care of what He gave you," he says. That philosophy was nurtured by his mother to encourage him as a boy growing up in poverty.

Robertson loved basketball but never took his game for granted. An intense competitor, he used awards as an incentive to improve. He challenged opponents to be at their best because he was "not afraid to fail." He believes that "if you are successful, you help other people." Evidence: he served for 11 years as President of the NBA's Players Union and since donating a kidney to his daughter Tia in 1997, has been active in the National Kidney Foundation's organ donor program.

Observers can learn but only doers accomplish.

Eight Steps to New Ideas

Every so often, it's easy to get the impression that one of your competitors has some secret source of ideas – some reservoir they can tap that gives them an advantage over you.

It's not true, of course, because everyone has the ability to originate ideas and solve problems. The process is rather simple. It is based on the way our minds combine ideas to create new ones.

Problem solutions and new ideas are created by recasting old experiences and manipulating old ideas. You combine them in new ways, put them in a new context of time or place, add other ideas, take something away, or change their meaning or purpose.

This process almost always is done deliberately and consciously.

> Winners recognize ideas which will create new opportunities. Losers choose those that create new problems.

The question is, do you go about this systematically? What process do you use to produce new ideas or to solve new problems?

Here are eight suggested steps:

1. **Name the target.** What's the problem? What kind of idea do you need?
2. **Get the facts.** Pile up all the information you can about the problem. This should include unsuccessful attempts to solve it. Often ideas that failed one time will, with a slight change, succeed at another time.
3. **Try the obvious solutions first.** Often merely naming a problem and collecting data about it will suggest solutions.
4. **Next: Try the wild ideas.** In particular, look for the apparently trivial, irrelevant aspects of the problem.
5. **Think intensely about the problem.** This is not really a separate step, but part of the steps we've mentioned before. Make yourself think about the problem until you have a

solution or until you've reached what might be called a state of frustration.

6. **Walk away from the problem.** Put it out of your conscious mind. At this point, if you have covered steps one through five, your subconscious will usually take over.
7. **Seize the flash of insight.** Generally, at some indefinite time after you walk away from the problem, you will find an answer welling up in your mind. Seize the idea at that moment and get it on paper.
8. **Do something about the idea.** And above all don't give up. We tend to get discouraged too easily. There are really easy ways to have good ideas, to solve tough problems. In the pursuit of an idea, the odds are all in favor of running into periods of discouragement when nothing goes right, when it appears that the answers will never come, when you begin to doubt the wisdom of what you are doing.

History is full of people who, through sheer determination, hung on through such periods – the Wright brothers, Alexander Bell, Morse, Edison. In my book, *Nothing Ventured, Nothing Gained,* I summarize many cases of living Americans. One of the most significant conclusions is that anyone who wants to try something new must go through disappointment and times when it seems much wiser to give up. The key is to persist in finding a better way.

Winners expand,
losers shrink.

Chapter 13

Measuring Progress

Expecting progress without measurement is at best deceptive, and at worst disastrous. The sooner in life we learn to look for tangible evidence the better we become. This chapter is devoted to ways and means of concentrating on objective (vs. subjective) evidence of improvement. It deserves special attention for ten simple, time tested reasons:

1. **Doing what works saves time and energy.**

   The ancient Romans were a good example. After suffering serious defeats, they copied the weapons and tactics of their enemies. Roman swords were adaptations of those used successfully by Spaniards. Roman armor was copied from Greeks who got more protection from what they wore. The breastplates used by Romans were too bulky, so they duplicated the more effective chain mail used by Gauls. The Roman navy was patterned after the galleys used by Carthaginians.

   History reveals that the Romans were successful because they learned from their mistakes and did not repeat them. But perhaps more importantly, they gained advantage by using the most successful techniques and equipment of all of their enemies.

> I don't want to do business with those who don't make a profit, because they can't give the best service.
>
> —William Bristol, co-founder, Bristol-Myers-Squibb Co.

2. Opinions without proof are hollow.

Larry Bossidy is perhaps the best known American executive who has specialized in "execution vs. big ideas." He believes in being realistic, removing opinions which are not supported and dropping excuses. His original executive experience was with General Electric where he rose to be Vice Chairman. His continuing focus on performance has enabled him to blend together the very different cultures of Allied Signal and Honeywell in recent years.

Bossidy believes that good companies are led by executives who are not easily swayed but constantly try to be objective about themselves and the accomplishments of their organizations. The bottom line of his belief is that "if we cannot prove we are getting better, the chances are we are going downhill."

•

Achievers look for facts, not opinion polls.

3. **Facts are more difficult to distort or hide.**

When Fred Smith was considering how to start a company he wanted to call Federal Express in the mid-1960's, he focused on the computer industry. He wondered what would happen if banks, for example, had to wait for snail mail to get the data they needed if their computers were down. The facts he gathered led him to meet that need with an overnight delivery service.

Smith formed a team which constructed a single system merging the use of planes and trucks into a nationwide network. His studies revealed that it had to be a complete system because if it was regional, he couldn't serve nationwide customers. That meant he had to put all of his eggs in one basket because his network had to be successful from day one.

He gave credibility to everyone involved by putting a lot of his own money on the line. His ambitious new system was a startling success and 26 months later, was operating with a profit. The stress on accountability has attracted and kept the people required for success. FedEx revenue in 2002 was $20.6 billion.

> The best leaders do not allow everything to be filtered. They frequently see for themselves.

4. Commitments to measurable goals are more visible to stakeholders.

Jeffrey Bleustein, the CEO of Harley Davidson, concentrates most of his attention on contacts with the people he believes are the keys to the company's success – customers, investors and employees. Bleustein attends most of the meetings of Harley Davidson owners, which are held throughout the country. He rides his motorcycle along with them. He gathers ideas for new products. He conducts an open meeting with employees annually in which suggestions are gathered from all 7,000 people. His frequent presence seems to say, "if these people don't think they know me, how could they ever believe that I would know what interests them?"

His frequent contact approach has paid off handsomely for Harley Davidson. In 1993, the company asked its unions for help in meeting a goal of selling 200,000 motorcycles a year by 2003. That's a tremendous increase from the 80,000 a year then produced. Amazingly, the goal was achieved 2 years early.

Feedback is a powerful motivator. For example, imagine your job is a bowling contest in which your boss is overlooking the pins on top of a curtain. Your boss can see the pins but you can't. You throw a ball and ask, "How many did I get?" and he says, "Adjust your stance." You try again and ask, "How did I do?" and he says, "Change your grip," so you try that and hear pins fall, and ask, "How am I doing?" He says, "Don't worry about it. We're going to have a meeting next week, and I'll tell you then." Sounds silly, but the sad fact is this type of "too little, too late" performance evaluation is rampant, anywhere we look.

> Truth has no special time of its own. Its hour is now – always.
>
> —Albert Schweitzer, theologian, missionary physician

5. **Requiring hard, cold evidence takes you out of your comfort zone.**

Robert L. Bailey is the CEO of PNC-Sierra, Inc. His performance motivator is simple. Every day during his commute to work, he imagines that he is about to be fired. The question he asks is, "What must I do today to save my job?" He has come up with some good answers because his company, which produces high-speed broadband microchips has enjoyed explosive growth. "We have to be bold," says Bailey. "We have to do things that clearly put us out of our personal comfort zones. If you're comfortable, that means you're not growing." Bailey's success did not come suddenly. He put in many 18-19 hour days while working on his graduate program when employed by Texas Instruments and AT&T. Two meals a day were provided by Denny's restaurants where he also worked during those years.

I have found in my consulting work over the years that the best organizations deliberately plan exit interviews with people who are leaving so that they can gather as many facts as possible about the reasons. I recommend you use the following questions to discover information that will be helpful in the future.

Exit Interview Questions

- Would you come back?
- What did you learn from working here?
- Do you feel your training was adequate for your position?
- Were you treated fairly?
- If you were not treated fairly, where was the treatment lacking?
- Was your opinion valued?
- If your opinion was not valued, in what specific areas were you ignored?

- What would you change about the operation?
- How would you describe your immediate supervisor?
- Who was your supervisor's manager?

6. **Even talented, highly motivated people cannot be satisfied with good intentions.**

Arthur Ashe would have been just another aspiring tennis player if he believed that racial prejudice would block his path. He overcame that temptation by believing that he would become so proficient, it would be impossible to keep him away.

By concentrating on his single objective of being the best tennis player in the world, he was able to maintain a consistent high-level of performance for 15 years. His refusal to be discouraged lasted until the premature end of his life after he was diagnosed with AIDS as a result of a contaminated blood transfusion during heart surgery.

Maury Wills did not make it to the major leagues until he had spent almost 9 years learning what he needed to know in the minors. Even baseball experts paid little attention to him because he was 5'8" tall and weighed only 150 lbs. Although scouts considered him to be a good runner and fielder, they thought he could not hit well enough to stay in the big leagues. He moved around the country for eight and a half years, kept his goals high and eventually made it with the Brooklyn Dodgers. Though he improved as a hitter, he determined that his greatest contribution could be as a base-stealer. He aimed to break the major league record, which had stood for almost fifty years. During the 1962 season, he broke Ty Cobb's record and was named the National League's most valuable player.

The Competitor's Creed

Talent is valuable but persistence is vital.

6. **"Busyness" will take over if there is no proof of progress.**

Lew Frankfort the Chairman and Chief Executive of Coach, Inc. takes nothing for granted. "To be successful," he says, "you need to live your business." He wants his executive team to have as many facts as they can gather to analyze market trends and evaluate the company's performance. He wants to do everything he can to reduce the risk of uncertainty in growing the company. To prove the point, Coach invests over $2 million a year on customer surveys alone.

To analyze reactions to Coach products, Frankfort visits stores every week to chat with customers. New products are tested extensively before being introduced. Weekly surveys are made to determine whether actual sales are different than projected by management.

> Brilliance accomplishes nothing
> until it is put to work.

7. **Facts tend to reduce the power of dominant leaders who preside over weak organizations and control individuals who believe they are victims.**

Too many organizations have to find out the hard way that there is danger at the top. When Boards of Directors are not conscientious and cautious they can find themselves selecting CEOs whose need for power is destructive. When self-confidence is carried to an extreme, it can yield an independence, which weakens organizations severely. Arrogance at any level is dangerous but in key positions it is a killer.

The highly regarded television executive Grant Tinker said it best.

> First we will be best,
> then we will be first.
>
> —Grant Tinker, T.V. Executive

But maybe the worst consequence of all when dominant leaders prevail is the fact that a victim attitude becomes rampant.

Who Are the Victims?

Everywhere you look are more victims. The people who say "I can't" have outnumbered the people who say "I will." We are drowning in needless pity for victims. Who is going to ask why? Why is dependence skyrocketing? Here are some clues:

- It is easier to find someone to blame for our own faults.
- Too many parents would rather work harder themselves to make things easier for their kids and the kids get lazier.
- Too many teachers feel unappreciated, and because they are protected by the tenure system, pass their resentments along to students.
- It is politically correct to advocate that everyone is entitled to anything they want and those who disagree are sexist, racist, capitalist egomaniacs.
- More and more institutions (private as well as public – commercial as well as not-for-profit) are thinking of themselves as having a welfare or rehabilitation mission.
- Colleges and Universities are focused on the credentialing process vs. stimulating people to "learn how to learn." Grade inflation detracts from the value of significant accomplishment. Too many degrees are granted automatically and

regarded by "graduates" as passports for privileges, or a substitute for proven performance.

8. Proof is the antidote for groundless opinions and guessing.

The best way to take guesswork out of any job is to prepare performance contracts. Why? Because *contracts create motivation for performance.*

- Making a contract with your boss cements your job commitments. You become *obligated* to achieve them. Your boss becomes *obligated* to support you.
- Contract-driven management opens options for new solutions. The "Whats" become more important than the "Hows."
- Performance Contracts provide boundaries for better management of our time and our work.
- Performance Contracts give meaning to our values. They go beyond good intentions and require action.
- Performance Contracts bring decisions into focus. Selecting alternatives becomes purposeful, easier and more accurate.
- Performance Contracts push us to overcome obstacles, adversity and opposition. They force us to recognize that it's a "What have you done for me *lately* world!"

- New contracts bring renewal. Bad habits can be dropped. Drifting can be replaced by measured progress.
- We grow with Performance Contracts and shrink in their absence. Competence without accomplishment is worthless.
- Performance Contracts provide both self rewards and self reprimands. You can develop a new boss – *Yourself!*
- Performance Contracts can be the essence of self control. Either you initiate them or someone else will.

> Honesty is not conditional.
> It depends only on telling the truth.

9. Trusting factual evidence provides the confidence to move on.

Winners know that the key to recovery is the ability to believe in and stay focused on the end goal. Dan Jansen found this out about himself in the 1994 Winter Olympics. At that time he had never won an Olympic gold medal. Soon after the start of his best race he almost fell and had to reach down and touch the ice to retain his balance. It was a mistake that would have cost most skaters a chance to win. But Jansen didn't falter. He didn't allow himself to be distracted. His instinct was to concentrate on his goal, not his mistake.

The key to recovery is to limit the effects of mistakes.

I am a firm believer in the fact that the most accurate reading of temperament is taken in bad times. The inclination to fall back as a result of a mistake, weakness or a temporary setback is conquered only by the discipline of damage control. That provides us with the ability to keep moving.

Olympic diver Michele Mitchell is another good example. In 1985, less than a year after she lost the gold medal to a Chinese diver, she found herself facing the same person in the World Cup final being held in China. As Mitchell prepared for her final dive, the Chinese audience grew silent, but as she approached the platform, they began making some of the loudest noises she had ever heard. Mitchell quickly realized that this was an attempt to distract her and she was not going to allow it. The result – a near perfect dive, which gave her the satisfaction that she had not only won the competition, she had overcome the pressure of the audience.

Two words make dreams become reality – Move It!

From Now On . . .
Position Yourself

To accomplish more, focus not on what you have done but what you have left to do.

I wish I could close with some type of guarantee. But I know it can't be done – and so do you. What I honestly believe is that by engaging yourself seriously in everything we have covered, you will, in fact, be able to *position yourself* to be more competitive for a long, long time. I can say this confidently because I have used these tools myself for many years as well as in thousands of situations with my clients.

Being competitive is more than a mindset. It is an underlying conviction which becomes a relentless commitment – a compulsion really – to apply the concepts and methods you believe in. As that happens, you will be rewarded as you find new ways to:

- **Anticipate change requirements.**
- **See new opportunities for growth.**
- **Gather evidence more objectively.**
- **Seek facts before opinions.**
- **Eliminate excuses to procrastinate.**

- **Avoid mistakes that hold you back.**
- **Resist temptations to allow mediocre performance.**
- **Face difficult decisions about people more realistically.**
- **Focus rewards on results instead of seniority, credentials or even "experience."**

I appreciate this opportunity to be on your side!

Index

Accomplishment *viii*, *xii*, 1, 5, 12, 16, 43, 45, 50, 55, 71, 74, 75, 82, 101, 115, 119, 126, 134, 142, 156, 157, 162, 169, 170, 172, 175
Accountability 2, 4, 5, 49, 50, 83, 135, 163
Achievers 8, 30, 32, 41, 43, 44, 45, 51, 63-64, 73, 80, 85, 88, 94, 98, 99, 101, 106, 114, 129, 139, 141, 146, 149, 163, 164, 171
Action *ix*, 3, 5, 8-10, 12, 13, 24, 25, 27, 36, 39, 42, 44-46, 50, 51, 67, 73, 75, 83, 101, 103, 106, 125, 127, 149, 150, 152, 155, 171
Action Plan 13, 44, 106, 150, 152, 155
Adversity 80, 97, 98, 103, 171
Adversity Quotient 97, 98
Advocates *ii*, 56, 170
Anger Control 33, 92, 94, 117, 123, 130
Authority *ix*, 9, 17, 110, 122, 136, 141
Behavior 15, 19, 20, 25, 33, 49, 50, 68, 82, 118
Blame 50, 51, 53, 123, 155, 170
Challenge *ix*, *xi*, 3, 7, 8, 25, 29, 33, 43, 49, 73-75, 90, 98, 121, 128, 142, 157
Change *x*, *xii*, 2, 3, 6, 7, 9, 15, 24, 30, 31, 32, 33, 37, 38, 39, 42-44, 46, 51, 65, 71, 72, 83, 87, 89, 98, 100, 103, 104, 112, 118-122, 125, 131-133, 139, 142, 157, 158, 165, 167, 175
Checkpoints 36, 43, 44
Coaching *ii*, 14, 35, 36, 75, 78, 104, 109, 148, 156, 168
Commitment *ii*, 5, 9, 12, 19, 25, 33, 35, 47, 63, 73, 74, 120, 150, 164, 171, 175
Communication 9, 12, 14, 125, 142, 151
Competitive Index 66
Confidence *xii*, 7, 33, 38, 50, 71, 73, 103, 108, 112, 121, 134, 140, 142, 169, 172, 175
Conflict 15, 25, 65, 85, 118, 147
Confrontation 15, 51, 76, 77
Consensus 12, 28
Credentials *ix*, 10, 50, 170, 176
Deadlines 37, 45, 47, 87, 97, 107, 118, 119
Decision-making 2, 10, 15, 21, 24, 26, 33, 38, 49, 55, 66, 68, 72, 73, 83, 86, 103, 119, 126, 133, 134-142, 156, 171, 176
Delegating 47, 67, 90, 133, 135, 136, 140, 141
Development 7, 9, 10-14, 23-26, 37, 39, 41, 44, 65, 79, 89, 96, 97, 98, 103, 109, 115, 120, 138, 139, 147, 172
Disagreement 2, 20, 23, 27, 51, 65, 68, 76, 106, 129, 141, 170
Effectiveness *xi*, 7, 9, 10, 14, 15, 21, 35, 36, 37, 39, 41, 44, 45, 64, 67, 68, 80, 118, 127, 133, 139, 140, 161
Efficiency 10, 48, 85, 122
Employees *ix*, *x*, 22, 54, 59-61, 65, 79, 81, 100, 109, 112, 115, 117, 119, 120, 129, 132, 135, 148, 164, 166
Evidence 2, 6, 31, 35, 49, 50, 53, 68, 69, 97, 157, 161, 165, 172, 175
Excuses 44, 53, 66, 67, 69, 162, 175
Exit Interview 166
Expectations 8, 20, 21, 22, 24-26, 31, 32, 62-64, 71, 80, 81, 85, 86, 91, 103, 121, 134, 142, 161
Expertise 51, 79, 82, 108, 109, 112, 147, 167
Facts 2, 10, 39, 41, 50, 65, 76, 83, 93, 94, 110, 118, 121, 146, 148, 158, 163, 165, 166, 168, 169, 172, 173, 175
Failure *x*, 2, 4, 6, 15, 37, 38, 39, 41, 44, 52, 54, 56, 69, 72, 86, 88, 90, 91, 93, 94, 95, 96, 97, 98, 99, 100, 112-118, 128, 133, 142, 143, 157, 158
Feedback 64, 86, 100, 165
Goals *xii*, 5, 8, 10, 27, 28, 33, 36, 38, 42, 49, 62, 63, 67, 71, 81, 88, 90, 98, 101, 106, 110, 112, 129, 134, 152, 155, 164, 167, 172
Growth 3, 7, 9, 25, 41, 43, 60, 61, 88, 89, 103, 104, 112-115, 128, 133, 141, 145, 156, 166, 168, 172, 175
Hiring and Firing *ii*, 3, 4, 51, 52, 53, 54, 55, 81, 101, 119, 120, 122, 132, 165
Ideas *xi*, 8, 9, 10, 22, 24, 25, 26, 27, 56, 62, 80, 81, 82, 96, 109, 124, 135, 149, 157-159, 162, 164
Inner Quest *viii*
Innovation 65, 82, 109

Integrity 55, 72
Key Factors 8
Leadership *ii, viii*, 4, 8, 9, 17, 18, 21, 23, 24, 26, 29, 41, 51, 55, 56, 62, 63, 64, 71, 75, 76, 81, 82, 91, 108, 109, 118, 125, 129, 133, 135, 136, 139, 141, 145, 164, 169
Liabilities 28, 96
Loyalty 4, 9, 60-62, 79, 129, 130, 142
Management *ii, x*, 1, 10, 12-14, 52, 63, 72, 121-124, 130, 135, 136, 138, 139, 148-152, 167, 169, 171
Managing Situations 15
Measurement *iv*, 10, 20, 40, 47, 62, 69, 117, 148, 161, 164, 172
Mission 12, 170
Motivation *xii*, 10, 14, 23, 26, 45, 62, 69, 75, 81, 129, 142, 165, 167, 171
Needs Analysis 28
Negotiation 10, 62, 68, 92, 96, 139
Objectives *xi*, 8, 9, 12, 13, 16, 18, 24, 25, 28, 30, 32, 39, 40, 41, 43, 44, 45, 68, 101, 139, 140, 146, 149, 167
Obstacles 33, 40, 97-99, 108, 114, 115, 171
Opinions 10, 28, 41, 59, 76, 77, 83, 125, 155, 162, 163, 166, 171, 175
Opponents 71, 73, 75, 80, 107, 157
Opportunities *iv*, 9, 25, 40, 41, 43, 52, 57, 67, 73, 78, 87, 89, 95, 97, 104, 107, 108, 112, 136, 158, 175, 176
Organization 1, 6, 7, 9, 10, 13, 18, 27, 28, 38, 49, 53, 54, 59, 62, 63, 68, 73, 81, 104, 121, 129, 136, 138, 139, 141, 145-147, 162, 166, 169
Performance *ii, ix*, 2, 4, 8-20, 22, 24, 36, 37, 47, 52, 53, 54, 59, 62, 64, 65, 67, 69, 86, 98, 99, 100, 101, 112, 116, 120, 121, 134, 136, 140, 148, 162, 165, 167, 168, 171, 172, 173, 176
Performance Appraisal 3, 89
Persistence *xi*, 48, 98, 137, 159, 168
Planning *xi*, 2, 4, 6, 8, 9, 12, 13, 17, 20, 27, 35, 36, 37, 38, 39, 40, 41, 42, 44-46, 48, 49, 68, 73, 79, 93, 106-108, 134, 150, 152, 155, 163, 166
Potential 13, 37, 54, 98, 115, 119, 129, 133
Pressure 5, 50, 65, 85, 86-90, 93, 106, 116-123, 126, 173
Pressure Quotient 116
Priorities 7, 12, 16, 27, 30, 33, 40, 44, 67, 72, 85, 90, 126, 150, 151, 155
Problem-solving 15, 145, 148, 149, 152
Progress *i, iv*, 9, 10, 12, 13, 36, 40, 45, 46, 62, 99, 110, 116, 142, 161, 168, 172
Proof 6, 31, 110, 125, 162, 168, 171
Rejection 91, 92-95, 98, 99, 128
Resources 12, 13, 42, 44, 51, 72, 139
Respect 4, 10, 23, 71, 77, 81, 110, 125
Results *xi*, 8, 10, 12, 17, 21, 27, 28, 31, 40, 43, 48, 62, 65, 85, 90, 101, 114, 118, 122, 124, 129, 139, 141, 167, 173, 176
Rewards 56, 65, 109, 172, 175, 176
Risk-taking 17, 24, 50, 55, 57, 68, 81, 94, 98, 118, 138, 139, 168
Ruler 23, 24, 25, 26
Sabotage 129, 130, 142
Self-appraisal 3
Seniority *ix*, 4, 10, 50, 176
Setbacks 90, 114, 116, 145, 173
Solutions 19, 44, 65, 80, 109, 112, 118, 137, 147, 149-152, 154, 155, 157-159, 171
Staffing 12, 13, 79, 131, 151
Strengths 13, 16, 18, 31, 33,-38, 53, 68, 119, 140
Stress *ix*, 53, 62, 66, 85, 88, 89, 90, 96, 108, 118, 119, 122, 163
Success *i, xi*, 2, 3, 6, 9, 34, 35, 39, 50, 52, 54, 56, 63-69, 73, 74, 77, 78, 81, 82, 90, 94, 95, 97-100, 103-105, 107, 110, 111, 114-116, 121, 128, 129, 135, 139, 143, 145, 146, 157, 158, 161-166, 168
Succession 13
Supervisors 9, 23, 37, 53, 59, 60-62, 64, 123, 130, 131, 134, 147, 167
Team building 52
Teamwork 14, 44, 51, 77
Tools *xi, xii*, 1, 4, 47, 151, 175
Trust 3, 14, 33, 51, 55, 80, 145, 172
Victims 169, 170
Weaknesses 3, 33, 36, 71, 107, 119, 140, 173